There is a river, the streams whereof shall make glad the city of God.

Psalm 46 vs. 4

The Little Red Bible of Jesus Christ's Teachings

The Little Red Bible of Jesus Christ's Teachings

The Words in Red

The Words of Christ in Red from the Holy Bible including a Special Section on the Prophecies of Christ's Coming and the End times

Brother William J. Sheehan L.M.T.

E-BookTime, LLC
Montgomery, Alabama

The Little Red Bible of Jesus Christ's Teachings
The Words in Red

ISBN: 978-1-60862-172-9

First Edition
Published May 2010
E-BookTime, LLC
6598 Pumpkin Road
Montgomery, AL 36108
www.e-booktime.com

From the Gospel of Saint Mark

From the Gospel of Saint John

The Acts of the Apostles

The Revelation of Saint John

Who is Jesus Christ According to the Scriptures?

Old Testament Prophecies of Jesus Christ and the New Testament Fulfillment

Foreword

This book is a compilation of the major teachings of Jesus Christ which are normally seen as the words in red within the pages of most Christian bibles which are in print today.

Although the entire word of God is precious to the Christian, there are times in my life when I find it comforting to read and to meditate on the words in particular of our Lord and Savior Jesus Christ.

I have taken the liberty of making some minor changes swapping out some of the Thees and Thous, and inserting some more commonly used words to make it a slightly easier read. This is actually the way I have learned to read the King James Version myself, making it in my opinion a little easier to understand.

Some of the readings are very brief. While others are quite lengthy. I did my very best to try not to tamper with what was printed in the Holy Scriptures. You will also find that additional scripture was added only where I felt that the particular quotation from Christ needed some supporting text in order to be better understood.

No one knows better than I the truth of God's word and the reality of his existence both yesterday, today and forever.

Myself, having had my own life saved not once but twice by his mercy. The first time was in my late teens by the Lord himself and then again in my early twenties by one of his angels.

Mary said at the wedding in Cana," whatever he tells you, do it." That being said, I am here to testify that we also should do whatever he tells us to do in his word, and that Jesus is faithful to do what he has said he will do. He is coming again. Are you ready?

From the Gospel of Saint Matthew

The Sermon on the Mount

Blessed are the poor in spirit: for theirs is the kingdom of heaven.

Blessed are they that mourn: for they shall be comforted.

Blessed are the meek; for they shall inherit the earth.

Blessed are they who do hunger and thirst after righteousness: for they shall be filled.

Blessed are the merciful: for they shall obtain mercy.

Blessed are the pure in heart: for they shall see God.

Blessed are the peacemakers: for they shall be called the children of God.

Blessed are they which are persecuted for righteousness sake: for theirs is the kingdom of Heaven.

Blessed are ye, when men shall revile you, and persecute you, and shall say all manner of evil against you falsely, for my namesake.

Rejoice and be exceeding glad; for great is your reward in heaven: for so they persecuted the prophets who were before you.

You are the salt of the earth: but if the salt has lost his savor, wherewith shall it be salted? It is therefore good for nothing but to be cast out, and to be trodden under foot of all men.

You are the light of the world. A city that is set on a hill cannot be hid. Neither do men light a candle and put it under a basket, but on a candlestick; and it gives light to all who are in the house.

Let your light so shine before men, that they may see your good works, and glorify your Father which is in heaven.

Think not that I have come to destroy the law, or the prophets: I have not come to destroy but to fulfill.

For truly I say to you, Till heaven and earth pass, one jot or one title shall in no way pass from the law, till all be fulfilled.

Whosoever shall therefore break one of the least of these commandments, and shall teach men to do so, he shall be called the least in the kingdom of heaven; but whoever shall do and teach them, the same shall be called great in the kingdom of heaven.

For I say unto you unless your righteousness exceeds the righteousness of the scribes and the Pharisees, you shall in no way enter into the kingdom of heaven.

You have heard that it was said by them of old time, you shall not kill; and whoever shall kill shall be in danger of the judgment.

But I say to you, that whoever is angry with his brother without a cause shall be in danger of the judgment; and whoever shall say to his brother Raca, shall be in danger of the council: but whoever shall say, You fool, shall be in danger of hell fire.

Therefore if you bring a gift to the altar, and there you remember that your brother has something against you;
Leave there your gift, before the altar, and go your way; first reconcile yourself with your brother, and then come and offer your gift.

Agree with your adversary quickly, while you are in the way with him; least at any time the adversary deliver you to the judge, and the judge delivers you to the officer, and you are then thrown into prison.

Truly I say to you, you shall in no way come out of there, until your have paid the uttermost farthing.

You have heard that it was said by them of old time, you shall not commit adultery:

But I say to you, whoever so much as looks at a woman and lusts after her has committed adultery already with her in his heart.

And if your right eye offends you, pluck it out and cast it away from you: for it is better for you that one of your members should perish, rather than your whole body be cast into hell fire.

And if your right hand offends you, cut it off and cast it away from you; for it is better for you that one of your members should perish and not that your whole body be cast into hell fire.

It has been said that whoever shall put away his wife, should give her a letter of divorce:

But I say to you, that whoever shall put away his wife except for the cause of fornication causes her to commit adultery: and whoever shall marry her that is divorced commits adultery also.

Again you have heard that it has been said of them of old time, you shall not swear yourself, but you shall perform to the Lord your oaths.

But I say to you, you shall not swear at all; neither by heaven; for it is God's throne; neither by the earth; for it is his footstool; neither by Jerusalem; for it is the city of the great King.

Neither shall you swear by your head, for you cannot make so much as one hair white or black.

But let your communications be yes or no, for anything more than this comes from the evil one.

You have heard that it has been said, an eye for an eye and a tooth for a tooth; But I say to you, that you should not resist evil; but whoever shall smite you on your right cheek, offer him your left also.

And if any man should sue you in court and take away your coat, offer him your cloak also.

And whoever compels you to go a mile with him, go with him two.

Give to him that asks something from you and to him that asks to borrow turn not yourself away.

You have heard that it has been said, love your neighbor and hate your enemy.

But I say to you, love your enemies, bless them that curse you, do good to them that hate you, and pray for them who despitefully use you.

That you may be the children of your Father which is in heaven: for he makes his sun to shine on the evil and on the good, and sends rain on the just and the unjust.

For if you love those who love you, what reward will you have? Do not even the publicans do the same thing?

And if you only salute your own brethren, what are you doing more than others do? Be ye therefore perfect even as your Father which is in heaven is perfect.

Take heed that you do not your good deeds before men to be seen of them: otherwise you have no reward of your father which is in heaven.

Therefore when you do your good deeds, do not sound a trumpet before you, as the hypocrites do in the synagogues and in the streets, that they may have glory of men. Truly I say to you, they have their reward.

But when you do good deeds, let not your left hand know what your right hand is doing. That your deeds may be in secret; and your Father which sees in secret himself shall reward you openly.

And when you pray you shall not be as the hypocrites are; for they love to pray standing in the synagogues and in the corners of the streets, that they may be seen of men. Truly I say to you, they have their reward.

But you when you pray enter into your closet, and when you have shut the door, pray to your Father which is in secret: and your Father which sees in secret shall reward you openly.

But when you pray use not vain repetitions, as the heathen do: for they think that they shall be heard for their much speaking.

Be you not therefore like them; for your Father knows what things you have need of, before you ask him. After this manner therefore you should pray.

****

The Our Father

Our Father which art in heaven, Hallowed be thy name. Thy kingdom come, Thy will be done in earth, as it is in heaven.

Give us this day our daily bread. And forgive us our debts as we forgive our debtors.

And lead us not into temptation, but deliver us from evil: for thine is the kingdom, and the power, and the glory, for ever. Amen

For if you forgive men their trespasses, your heavenly Father will also forgive you: But if you forgive not men their trespasses, neither will your Father forgive your trespasses.

Moreover when you fast, be not as the hypocrites, of a sad countenance: for they disfigure their faces that they may appear to men to be fasting. Truly I say to you that they have their reward.

But you, when you fast, anoint your head and wash your face that you do not appear to men to be fasting; and your Father which sees in secret shall reward you openly.

Lay not up for yourselves treasures on earth, where moths and rust do corrupt them, and where thieves break in and steal. For where your treasure is there will your heart be also.

The light of the body is the eye; if therefore the eye be evil, the whole body shall be full of darkness. If therefore the light that is in you be in darkness, how great is that darkness!

No man can serve two masters: for he will either hate the one and love the other: or else he will hold on to one, and despise the other. You cannot serve both God and money.

Therefore I say to you, take no thought for your life, what you shall eat, and what you shall drink; neither for your body, what you shall put on it.

Is not your life more than meat, and the body more than what you wear?

Behold the birds of the air: for they neither sow seeds, neither do they reap a harvest: yet your heavenly Father feeds them. Are you not much better than they are?

Which of you by taking thought can add so much as one foot to his stature?

And why do you take any thought about clothing? Consider the lilies of the field: how they grow; they toil not, neither do they spin.

And yet I say to you, that even Solomon in all his glory was not arrayed like one of these.

If God therefore so clothes the grass of the field, which today is and tomorrow is cast into the oven shall he not much more clothe you, you of little faith?

Therefore take no thought saying, What shall we eat? or What shall we drink? Or with what shall we be clothed?

For all these things do the gentiles seek; for your heavenly Father knows that you have need of all these things.

But seek you first the kingdom of God and his righteousness: and all these things shall be added to you.

Take no thought therefore for tomorrow: for tomorrow will take care of the things for itself. Sufficient for today is the evil contained in it.

My Prayer.....Lord help me this day to trust in your promises that you will provide the things that I have need of this day and every day....Amen

****

The Sermon on the Mount Continued

Judge not that you be not judged. For with what judgment you judge, you shall be judged: and with whatever measure you judge, it will be measured to you also.

And why do you behold the speck that is in your brothers eye, but you consider not the beam that is in your own?

Or how can you say to your brother, let me pull out the speck that is in your eye; and behold a beam is in your own.

You hypocrite, first take the beam out of your own eye; and then you shall be able to see clearly to help your brother to take the speck out of his own eye.

Give not that which is holy to the dogs, neither throw your pearls before swine, for they will trample them under their feet and turn at you to tear you to pieces.

Ask and it will be given to you; seek and you will find; and to him that knocks the door will be opened for him.

For everyone who asks receives, and he that seeks finds, and to him that knocks it shall be opened.

Or what man is there among you who if his son asks him for bread will he give him a stone? Or if he asks him for a fish will he give him a serpent?

If you then being evil know how to give good gifts to your children, how much more shall your Father which is in heaven give good things to them that ask of him.

Therefore all things you would like men to do to you, you do the same for them; for this is the entirety of the law and the prophets.

Enter in at the strait gate; for wide is the gate, and broad is the way that leads to destruction, and many there be that go in there.

Because strait is the gait, and narrow is the way, which leads to eternal life, and few there be that find it.

Beware of false prophets that come to you in sheep's clothing, but inwardly they are ravaging wolves.

You will know them by their fruits. Do men gather grapes out of thorn bushes, or figs from thistles?

Even so every good tree brings forth good fruit; but a corrupt tree brings forth evil fruit. A good tree cannot bring forth bad fruit neither can a corrupt tree bring forth good fruit.

Every tree that brings forth not good fruit will be cut down and cast into the fire. Wherefore by their fruits you shall know them.

Not everyone that says to me, Lord, Lord, shall enter into the kingdom of heaven; but those who do the will of my Father which is in heaven.

Many will say to me in that day, Lord, Lord, have we not prophesied in your name and in your name have we not cast out devils? And in your name done many wonderful works?

And then I will profess to them, I never knew you, depart from me you that work at iniquity.

Therefore whoever hears these sayings of mine and does them, I will take him as being a wise man who built his house upon a rock.

And the rains descended and the floods came and the winds blew, and beat upon that house; and it did not fall, for it was built upon a rock.

And everyone who hears these sayings of mine and does not do them shall be like a foolish man, which built his house upon the sand.

And the rains descended and the floods came, and the winds blew, and beat upon that house, and it fell; and great was the fall of it.

My Prayer….. Lord may I always stand in your strength. For when I am weak you are surely strong…Amen

****

Healing the Leper

And there came a leper who was worshiping Christ and said to him; Lord if you will you can make me clean. And Jesus put forth his hand and said to him; I will, be thou clean. And immediately he was cleansed of the leoprosy. Jesus then said; See that you tell no man; but go your way, show yourself to the priest, and offer the gift that Moses commanded, for a testimony unto them.

****

The Centurions Servant is Healed

And while Jesus was at Capernaum a centurion came to him saying, Lord my servant is at home grievously tormented of the palsy. And Jesus said I will come and heal him. With that the soldier said; Lord it is not necessary for you to come but only speak the word and it shall be done.

He then said that he also was a man with authority, having soldiers under him. And I say to this one, Go, and he goes, and to another, Come and he comes. And Jesus said; Truly I say unto you, I have not found so great a faith in all of Israel. And I say to you, that many shall come from the east and from the west and shall sit down with Abraham, and with Isaac, and with Jacob, in the kingdom of heaven.

But the children of the kingdom shall be cast out into outer darkness; there shall be weeping and gnashing of teeth. Christ then said to the centurion; Go your way, and as you have believed, so be it done to you…his servant was healed.

****

His Followers are Tested

A certain scribe came to him and said; Master, I will follow you wherever you go. And Jesus said to him; The foxes have holes, and the birds of the air have nests; but the Son of man has no where to lay down his head. Then another one of his disciples said to him; Lord let me first go and bury my dead, and then I will follow you. And Jesus said to him;

Follow me and let the dead bury their dead.

****

Healing the Palsied Man

He said to the man; Son, be of good cheer thy sins be forgiven the. The Jews hearing this said to themselves; Who is he that he thinks he has the power to forgive sins? And Jesus said; Wherefore do you think evil in your hearts?

For which is easier to say, Thy sins be forgiven you; or to say Arise and walk?

But that you may know that the Son of man has power on earth to forgive sins, he said to the man; Arise take up your bed, and go to your house.

****

The Question of Eating with Sinners

And it came to pass that Christ and his apostles sat in a house and had dinner with many sinners and publicans. And when the Pharisees saw this they said to his disciples; Why does your master eat with sinners and publicans? Jesus, hearing what they said told them; They that are well do not need a physician, but those that are sick. But you go and find out what that means; I will have mercy and not sacrifice; for I have not come to call the righteous but rather sinners to repentance.

****

Why His Followers do Not Fast Often

Can the children of the bride chamber mourn as long as the bridegroom is with them? But the days are coming when the bridegroom shall be taken from them, and then they shall fast.

No man puts a piece of new cloth into an old garment. For that which is put in it to fill the tear takes from the garment, and the rent is made worse.

Neither do men put new wine in old bottles; else the bottles break, and the wine runs out, and the bottles perish; but they put new wine in new bottles, and both are preserved.

****

The Harvest

The harvest truly is plentiful, but the laborers are few; Pray therefore to the Lord of the harvest; that he will send forth laborers into the harvest.

****

The Twelve Apostles are Sent

Go not into the way of the Gentiles, and into any city of the Samaritans enter not.

But go rather to the lost sheep of the house of Israel. And as you go, preach saying, the kingdom of heaven is at hand.

Heal the sick, cleanse the lepers, raise the dead, cast out devils; freely you have received, freely give.

Carry neither gold, nor silver, nor brass in your purses, nor scrip for your journey, neither carry two coats, nor shoes, nor staves; for the workman is worthy of his meat.

And in whatever city or town you enter into; enquire who in it is worthy; and there abide until you leave there.

And when you come into a house salute it. And if the house be worthy let your peace come upon it, but if not worthy, let your peace return to you.

And whoever shall not receive you, nor hear your words, when you depart from that house or city, shake off the dust of your feet.

For truly I say to you, it shall be more tolerable for Sodom and Gomorrah in the day of judgment than for that house or city.

Behold I send you forth as sheep in the midst of wolves; be you therefore wise as serpents, and harmless as doves.

But beware of men; for they will deliver you up to the council, and they will scourge you in their synagogues.

And you shall be brought before governors and kings for my namesake, and for a testimony against them and the Gentiles.

But when they deliver you up, take no thought of how or what you shall speak; for it will be given to you in that same hour what you shall speak.

For it is not you that speak but the Spirit if your Father that speaks in you.

And brother shall deliver brother unto death, and the father the child; and the children shall rise up against their parents, and cause them to be put to death.

And you shall be hated of all men for my names sake; but he that endures to the end shall be saved.

But when they persecute you in this city, flee into another; for truly I say unto you, you shall not have gone over the cities of Israel, until the Son of man has come.

The disciple is not above his master, or the servant greater that his lord. It is enough for the disciple that he is as his master, and the servant as his lord? If they have called the master of the house the devil, how much more shall they call them of his household?

Fear them not therefore; for there is nothing covered, that shall not be revealed; and hid that shall not be known.

What I tell you in darkness that you shall speak in the light; and what you hear in the ear, that speak you on the housetops.

And fear not them which kill the body, but are not able to kill the soul; but rather fear him who is able to destroy both body and soul in hell.

Are not two sparrows sold for a farthing? And one of them shall not fall to the ground without your Father knowing it. But the very hairs of your head are numbered.

Fear not therefore, you are of greater value than many sparrows. Whoever therefore shall confess me before men, him will I confess also before my Father which is in heaven.

But whoever will deny me before men, him also will I deny before my Father which is in heaven.

Think not that I have come into the world to bring peace; I came not to send peace, but a sword.

For I have come to set at variance a man against his father, and the daughter against her mother, and the daughter in-law against her mother in law. And a mans foes shall be they of his own household.

He that loves father or mother more than me is not worthy of me. And he that's takes not up his cross and follows after me is not worthy of me.

He that finds his life shall lose it, and he that lose his life for my sake shall find it.

He that receives you receives me, and he that receives me receives him that sent me. He that receives a prophet in the name of a prophet shall receive the prophet's reward.

And whoever shall give to drink a cup of water to one of these little ones only in the name of a disciple shall in no way lose his reward.

My Prayer.....Help me this day and every day Lord to be faithful as were your apostles to that which you have called me to do…Amen

****

The Question from John the Baptist

Go and show John again the things which you both hear and see.

The blind receive their sight and the lame walk, the lepers are cleansed and the deaf hear, the dead are raised up and the poor have the gospel preached to them.

And blessed is he whoever shall not be offended in me. What did you go out into the wilderness to see? A reed shaken in the wind? But what did you go out to see?

A man clothed in soft raiment? Behold they that wear soft clothing are in king's houses.

But what did you go out to see? A prophet? Yes and much more than a prophet.

For this was he of whom it is written, Behold I send my messenger before thy face, which shall prepare thy way before you.

Truly I say before you, among them that have been born of women there has not been a greater than John the Baptist; not withstanding, he that is least in the kingdom of heaven is greater than he.

And from the days of John the Baptist until now, the heavens suffer violence and the violent take it by force.

For all the prophets and the law prophesied before John And if you will receive it, this was Elias which was said to come. He that has ears to hear let him hear.

But to what shall I compare this generation. It is like children sitting in the market and calling to their fellows, And saying we have piped to you, and you have not danced; we have mourned to you and you have not lamented.

For John came neither eating nor drinking and they say he has a devil.

The Son of man came both eating and drinking and they say behold a gluttonous man and a wine bibber, a friend of the publicans and sinners. But wisdom is justified of her children.

Woe unto you Chorazin! Woe unto you Bethsaida! For if the mighty works which were done in you, had been done in Tyre and Sidon, they would have repented long ago in sackcloth and ashes.

But I say unto you it shall be more tolerable for Tyre and Sidon then for you in the day of judgment.

And you Capernaum which are exalted unto heaven shall be brought down to hell; for if the mighty works which were done in thee had been done in Sodom, it would have remained until this day.

But I say unto you, it shall be more tolerable for Sodom in the day of judgment then for you.

I thank you oh Father, Lord of heaven and earth, that you have hid these things from the wise and the prudent, and have revealed them to babes.

Even so father, for though it seemed good in your sight. All things are delivered unto me of my Father; and no man knows the Son but the Father.

Neither does any man know the Father except the Son, and he to whoever the Son reveals him.

Come unto me all you who labor and are heavy laden and I will give you rest.

Take my yoke upon you and learn of me; For I am meek and lowly of heart; and you shall find rest in your souls. For my yoke is easy and my burden is light.

****

Christ's Teaching on the Sabbath

Have you not read what David did and they that were with him were hungry?

How he entered into the house of God and did eat the showbread, which was not lawful for him to eat, or for those who were with him, but only for the priests.

Or have you not read in the law, how that on the Sabbath days the priests profane the Sabbath and are blameless? But I say to you in this place is one greater than the temple.

But if you had known what this means, I will have mercy and not sacrifice, you would not have condemned the guiltless. For the Son of man is Lord even of the Sabbath day.

What man is there among you, that has one sheep, and if it falls into a pit on the Sabbath day will not grab hold of it and pull it out?

How much better than is a man than a sheep? Therefore is it lawful to do well on the Sabbath day?

Every kingdom divided against itself is brought to desolation; and every city or house divide against itself shall not stand.

And if Satan casts out Satan, he is divided against himself; how then can his kingdom stand?

And if the devil is cast out by devils, by whom then do your children cast them out? Therefore they shall be your judges.

But if I cast out devils by the spirit of God, then the kingdom of God has come among you.

Or else how can someone enter into a strong mans house and rob his goods, unless he first binds the strong man, and then he can enter and rob his house.

He that is not with me is against me, and he that gathers not with me scatters abroad.

Therefore I say unto you, all manner of sin and blasphemy shall be forgiven men; but blasphemy against the Holy

Ghost, it shall not be forgiven him, neither in this world or in the world to come.

And whoever speaks a word against the Son of man, it shall be forgiven him; but whoever speaks a word against the Holy Ghost, it shall not be forgiven him, neither in this world or the world to come.

Either make the tree good and its fruit good, or make the tree corrupt and its fruit corrupt. For the tree shall be known by its fruit.

Oh you generation of vipers, how can you being evil speak good things? For out of the abundance of the heart the mouth speaks.

A good man out of the good treasure of his heart brings forth good things; and an evil man out of the evil treasure brings forth evil things.

For by your words you shall be justified and by your words you shall be condemned.

****

Those Seeking a Sign

An evil and adulterous generation seeks after a sign; and there shall no sign be give to it, but the sign of the prophet Jonas.

For as Jonas was three days and three nights in the whales belly; so shall the Son of man be three days and three nights in the heart of the earth.

The men of Nineveh shall rise in judgment with this generation, and shall condemn it because they repented at the preaching of Jonas; and behold a greater than Jonas is here.

The queen of the south shall rise up in judgment with this generation and shall condemn it; for she came from the uttermost parts of the earth to hear Solomon's wisdom; and behold a greater than Solomon is here.

When the unclean spirit is gone out of a man, he walks through dry places seeking rest, and finds none.

Then he says I will return to my house from where I came out; and when he has come, he finds it empty, swept, and garnished.

Then he goes in, and takes with himself seven other spirits more wicked than himself, and they enter in and dwell there; and the last state of the man is worse than the first.

Even so shall it be also unto this wicked generation.

Who is my mother? And who are my brethren! Behold my mother and my brethren!

For whoever shall do the will of my Father which is in heaven, the same is my brother, and sister, and mother.

My prayer....Lord may your Holy Spirit dwell within me always, and may my tongue speak words of your wisdom to those who are put before me each day...Amen

****

The Seven Parables of Christ

Behold a sower went forth to sow; And when he sowed some seeds fell by the way side, and the fowls came and devoured them up.

Some fell upon stony places, where they had not much earth; and quickly they sprang up because they had no depth of soil.

And when the sun was up they were scorched; and because they had no root they withered away.

And some fell among thorns; and the thorns sprung up and choked them out.

But others fell unto good ground and brought forth fruit, some a hundred fold, some sixty fold, and some thirty fold. Whoever has ears to hear let him hear.

Because it is given to you to know the mysteries of the kingdom of heaven, but to them it is not given.

For whoever has to him shall be given, and he shall have more abundance; but to him who has not, from him shall be taken from even that which he has.

Therefore speak I to them in parables; because in seeing they see not; and in hearing they hear not; neither do they understand.

And in them is fulfilled the prophecy of Isaiah, which says, By hearing you shall hear and not understand; and seeing you shall see and not perceive.

For this peoples heart has waxed gross, and their ears are dull of hearing, and their eyes they have closed.

Lest at any time they should see with their eyes, and hear with their ears, and should understand with their heart, and should be converted and I should heal them.

Hear you therefore the parable of the sower. When anyone hears the word of the kingdom, and understands it not, then comes the wicked one and catches away that which was sown in his heart.

This is he which received the seed by the way side. But he that received the seed in stony places, the same is he that receives the word with great joy.

Yet has no root in himself, but endures for a while; for when tribulation and persecution arise because of the word, by and by he is offended.

He also that receives seed among thorns, is he that hears the word; and the cares of this world and the deceitfulness of riches, choke the word and he becomes unfruitful.

But he that receives the word in good ground, is he that hears the word and receives it; which also bears fruit, and brings forth some a hundredfold, some sixty, and some thirty.

The kingdom of heaven is likened to a man that sowed good seed into his field. But while the man slept his enemy came and sowed tares in among the wheat, and went his way.

But when the blades had sprung up and brought forth fruit, there the tares appeared also.

So the servants of the householder came to him and said him, Sir, Did you not sow good seed in your field? Where than did these tares come from?

He said to them, an enemy has done this. The servants said to him, would you have us go and gather them up? But he said no. Because when you are gathering up the tares you may pull up the wheat with them.

Let both grow together until the time of the harvest; and at the time of the harvest I will say to the reapers; Gather together first the tares and bundle them together to be thrown into the fire; but gather the wheat into my barn.

The kingdom of heaven is like a grain of mustard seed, which a man took and sowed into his field.

Which indeed is the least of all seeds; but when it is grown, it is the greatest among herbs, and becomes a tree so that the birds of the air come and lodge in its branches.

The kingdom of heaven is like leaven, which a woman took, and hid in three measures of meal, until the whole was leavened.

He that sows the good seed is the Son of man. The field is the world; the good seed are the children of the kingdom; but the tares are the children of the wicked one.

The enemy that sowed them is the devil; and the harvest is the end of the world; and the reapers are the angels of God.

As therefore the tares are gathered together and burned in the fire, so shall it be at the end of this world.

The Son of man shall send forth angels, and they shall gather all things out of his kingdom that are found to be offensive, and those which do iniquity.

And shall cast them into a furnace of fire; there shall be wailing and gnashing of teeth.

Then shall the righteous shine forth as the sun in the kingdom of their Father. Who has ears to hear let him hear.

Again the kingdom of heaven is like a treasure hidden in a field; which when a man has found it ,he hides it again, and for the joy thereof, goes and sells all that he has to buy that field.

Again the kingdom of heaven is like a merchant man who is seeking to buy good pearls, Who when he had found one pearl of great price, went and sold all that he had and bought it.

Again the kingdom of heaven is like a net that was cast into the sea and gathered up some of every kind.

Which when it was full they drew to the shore, and sat down, and gathered the good into vessels and cast the bad away.

So shall it be at the end of the world; the angels shall come forth and sever the wicked from among the just.

And shall cast them into the furnace of fire; there shall be wailing and gnashing of teeth. Jesus then said to them, Have you understood all of these things?

Therefore every scribe who is instructed about the kingdom of heaven is like a man that is a householder, which brings forth out of his treasure things new and old.

A prophet is not without honor, except in his own country, and in his own household.

My Prayer… Thank you Lord for that pearl of great price, which is you. May I by your Spirit remain faithful to your word… Amen

****

The Pharisees are Reproved by Christ

Why do you also transgress the commandment of God by your tradition? For God commanded, saying, Honor thy father and thy mother; and, he that curses his father or mother let him die the death.

But you say, whoever shall say to his father or his mother, it is a gift by whatever you may be profited by me. And honor not his father or his mother, he shall be free.

Thus you have made the commandment of God of no effect by your tradition.

You hypocrites, well did Isaiah prophesy of you in saying, this people draw nigh to me with their mouth, and honor me with their lips; but their heart is far from me.

But in vain do they worship me teaching for doctrine the commandments of men.

Hear and understand. Its not that which goes into the mouth that defiles a man; but that which comes out of the mouth, this is what defiles a man.

Every plant which my heavenly Father has not planted shall be rooted up. Let them alone; they be blind leaders of the blind and both shall fall into the ditch.

Are you also still without understanding? Do you not yet understand that whatever enters into the mouth goes into the belly, and is cast out into the draught.

But those things which proceed forth out of the mouth come from the heart; and they defile the man.

For out of the heart proceed evil thoughts, murders, adulteries, fornications, thefts, false witness and blasphemies.

These are the things which defile a man; but to eat with unwashed hands defiles not a man.

****

Sign Seekers are Again Rebuked

When it is evening, you say, it will be fair weather for the sky is red. And in the morning it will be foul weather for it is red and lowring.

Oh you hypocrites, you can discern the face of the sky; but you cannot discern the signs of the times.

A wicked and an adulterous generation seeks after a sign and there shall no sign be given unto it, but he sign of the prophet Jonas.

Take heed and beware of the leaven of the Pharisees and of the Sadducees.

Oh you of little faith, why do you reason amongst yourselves because you have brought no bread?

Do you not yet understand nor yet remember the five loaves and the five thousand , and how many baskets you took up?

How is it that you do not understand that I spoke it to you not concerning bread that you should beware of the leaven of the Pharisees and of the Sadducees?

Who do men say that I the Son of man am? And who do you say that I am? Peter said, you are the Christ, the Son of the living God.

Blessed are you Simon Barjona; for flesh and blood has not revealed this to you, but my Father which is in heaven.

And I say unto you that you are Peter, and upon this rock I will build my church; and the gates of hell shall not prevail against it.

And I will give to you the keys to the kingdom of heaven; and whatever you shall bind on earth shall be bound in heaven; and whatever you shall loose on earth shall be loosed in heaven.

****

Peter Tells Christ Not to Go to Jerusalem

Get thee behind me, Satan; you are an offense to me; for you savor not the things that be of God, but those things that be of men.

If any man will come after me, let him deny himself, pick up his cross, and follow me.

For whoever will save his life shall loose it, and whoever will loose his life for my sake shall find it.

For how is a man profited if he shall gain the whole world and loose his soul? Or what shall a man give in exchange for his soul?

For the Son of man shall come in the glory of his Father with his angels; and then he shall reward every man according to his works.

Truly I say unto you there shall be some standing here, which shall not taste of death until they see the Son of man coming in his kingdom.

****

The Transfiguration

Jesus had taken some of the disciples up to a high mountain and was transfigured before them; and his face shined like the sun and his clothing was as white as the light. And there appeared Moses and Elias talking with Christ. And after they saw this they fell to the ground. He said to them; Arise and be not afraid. Tell the vision to no man, until the Son of man be raised again from the dead.

Elias shall truly come first, and restore all things. But I say unto you, that Elias has come already, and they knew him not, but have done to him whatever they wanted.

Likewise also shall the Son of man also suffer of them.

****

The Healing of the Demonic Man

After the demons would not obey the apostles and come out of the man, Jesus said to them; Oh faithless and perverse generation, how long shall I be with you? How long shall I suffer with you? Bring him here to me.

He said to them; Because of your unbelief the demons came not out of him, for truly I say unto you, if you have faith as a grain of mustard seed, you shall say to this mountain, remove yourself from here and go over yonder, and it shall be removed.

And nothing shall be impossible for you, however this kind of demon goes out by prayer and fasting only.

****

Tribute Money

The Son of man shall be betrayed into the hands of men; and they shall kill him and he shall be raised again the third day. What do you think Simon?

Of whom do the kings of the earth take custom or tribute? Of their own children or strangers? Peter said of strangers. The Lord said, Then are the children free?

Not withstanding so we do not offend them, you go to the sea and cast a hook, and take up the first fish that you catch, and when you shall open his mouth you shall find a piece of money; that take and give to them for me and you.

****

Little Children

Truly I say unto you, except you become converted and be as little children, you shall not enter into the kingdom of heaven.

Whoever therefore shall humble himself and become as this little child, the same is greatest in the kingdom of heaven.

And whoever receives such a little one as this child, receives me.

But whoever shall offend one of these little ones which believes in me, it would be better for him if a mill stone was hung around his neck and that he was then cast into the sea.

Woe be it to the world because of its offenses! For offences must come, but woe to that man by whom the offense comes.

Therefore if your hand or your foot offends you, cut them off and cast them away from you, It is better for you to enter into life halt or maimed, then to have two hands and two feet and to be cast into eternal fire.

And if your eye offends you, pluck it out and cast it away from you, for it is better for you to enter into life with one eye, than to have two eyes and to be cast into hell fire.

Take heed that you despise not one of these little ones; for I say to you that in heaven their angels do always behold the face of my Father which is in heaven.

For the Son of man has come to save that which is lost. How do you think?

That if a man shall have a hundred sheep, and one of them has gone astray, does he not leave the ninety nine and go into the mountains to find the one which is lost?

And if it be that he finds it, he rejoices more over that one sheep than of the ninety nine which were not lost.

Even so it is the will of your Father which is in heaven, that not one of these little ones should perish.

Moreover if your brother shall trespass against you, go and tell him his fault between you and him alone; if he shall hear you, you have gained your brother.

But if he will not hear you, than take with you one or two more that in the mouth of two or more witnesses every word may be established.

And if he shall neglect to hear them, tell it to the church, let him be to you as a heathen man and a publican.

Truly I say to you, whatever you shall bind on earth shall be bound in heaven, and whatsoever you shall loose on earth shall be loosed in heaven.

Again I say to you that if two of you shall agree as touching anything they shall ask, it shall be done for them of my Father which is in heaven.

For where to or three are gathered together in my name, there I am in the midst of them.

****

Unlimited Forgiveness

I say not to you, you shall forgive seven times; but, seventy times seven.

Therefore is the kingdom of heaven like a certain king that would take an account of his servants

And when he had begun to reckon, one was brought to him who owed him ten thousand talents.

But inasmuch as he had nothing to pay, his lord commanded him to be sold, his wife, and children, and all that he had, and payment to be made.

The servant therefore fell down and worshipped him, saying, lord have patience with me and I will repay you all.

Then the lord of that servant was moved with compassion, and loosed him, and forgave him the debt.

But the same servant went out, and found one of his fellow servants, which owed him a hundred pence; and he layed his hands on him, and took him by the throat saying, pay me what you owe me.

And his fellow servant fell down at his feet saying, have patience with me and I will repay you all that I owe.

And he would not allow him to do so but took him and cast him into prison until he should repay all.

So when his fellow servants saw this, they were very sad, and went to their lord and told him all that was done.

Then his lord after he had called him, said to him, Oh you wicked servant, I forgave you all your debt because you asked me.

Should you not also have had compassion on your fellow servant, even as I had pity on you?

And his lord was angry, and delivered him to the tormentors until he should pay all that was due to him.

So likewise shall my heavenly Father do also unto you, if you from your hearts forgive not every one his brother his transgressions.

****

Marriage is Sacred

Have you not read that he which made them in the beginning made them male and female?

And said for this cause shall a man leave father and mother, and shall cleave to his wife; and the two shall be one flesh. Wherefore they are no longer two but one flesh.

What therefore God has joined together let no man break apart.

Moses because of the hardness of your hearts suffered you to put away your wives; but from the beginning it was not so.

And I say to you, whoever shall put away his wife except it be for fornication, and shall marry another, commits adultery, and whoever does marry her that was put away does commit adultery.

All men cannot receive this saying, save those to whom it is given.

For there are some eunuchs which were so born from the womb; and there be some eunuchs which were made so of men; and there are eunuchs which made themselves eunuchs for the kingdom of heaven sake.

He that is able to receive it let him receive it. Suffer little children, and forbid them not to come to me; for of such is the kingdom of heaven.

****

Perfection and the Question of Riches

Why do you call me good? There is none good but one, that is God; but if you will enter into life, keep the commandments.

You shall not commit murder, you shall not commit adultery, you shall not steal, you shall not bear false witness, honor your father and mother; and you shall love your neighbor as yourself.

To the rich young man he said. If you want to be perfect, go and sell all that you have and give it to the poor, and you shall have treasure in heaven; and come and follow me.

Truly I say to you that a rich man shall hardly enter in to the kingdom of heaven.

And again I say to you that it is easier for a camel to go through the eye of a needle, than for a rich man to enter the kingdom of God.

With men this is impossible, but, with God all things are possible.

****

Parable of the Vineyard

Truly I say to you, that you which have followed me in the regeneration when the Son of man shall sit in the throne of his glory, you also shall sit upon twelve thrones, judging the twelve tribes of Israel.

And everyone that has forsaken houses, or brethren, or sisters or brothers or mother or wife or children or lands for my namesake, shall receive a hundredfold and shall inherit eternal life.

For the kingdom of heaven is like a man who is a householder, which went out early in the morning to hire laborers to work in his vineyard.

And when he had agreed with the laborers for a penny a day, he sent them into his vineyard.

And he went out again about the third hour and he saw others standing idle in the marketplace. And he said to them; you go also into the vineyard, whatever is right I will give to you.

And they went their way. Again he went out at the sixth and the ninth hour and did the same thing.

And again at the eleventh hour he went out, and found others standing idle, and he said to them, why do you stand here all the day idle?

They said to him, because no man has hired us. He said to them, you go also into the vineyard and whatever is right you shall receive.

So when evening had come, the lord of the vineyard said to his steward, call the laborers and give them their wages beginning from the last to the first.

And when those came that were hired at the eleventh hour they received a penny each.

But when the first came, they supposed that they should receive more; but they likewise received a penny.

And when they received it they murmured against the goodman of the house.

Saying, these last ones have worked but one hour and you have paid them equal to us, which have bourn the burden of the heat of the day.

But he answered one of them and said, friend I do you no wrong; did you not agree to work with me for a penny?

Take what is yours and go your way; and I will give to these last the same as you. Is it not lawful for me to do what I will with my own?

Is your eye evil because I am good? So the last shall be first and the first shall be last; for many are called but few are chosen.

****

Suffering and Human Ambition

Behold we go up to Jerusalem; and the Son of man shall be betrayed to the chief priests and to the scribes, and they shall condemn him to death.

And shall deliver him to the Gentiles to mock, and to scourge, and to crucify him; and the third day he shall rise again.

Then came the mother of Zebedee and asked if her two children could sit on his right and left hand in heaven.

You know not what you ask. Are you able to drink of the cup that I shall drink of, and to be baptized with the baptism that I am baptized with?

You shall indeed drink of my cup and be baptized with my baptism, but to sit on my right hand and on my left is not mine to give, but it shall be given to them for whom it is prepared of my Father in heaven.

****

The Spiritual Kingdom

You know that the princes of the Gentiles exercise dominion over them, and them that are great exercise authority over them.

But it shall not be so with you; whoever will be great among you let him be your minister; and whoever will be chief among you let him be your servant.

Even as the Son of man came not to be ministered to; but to minister, and to give his life as a ransom for many.

****

His Entry into Jerusalem

Go into the village over against you, and immediately you will find an ass tied, and a colt with her; loose them and bring them to me.

And if any man says anything to you, you shall say, The Lord has need of them; and straightway he will send them.

****

The Temple

It is written, my house shall be called a house of prayer, but you have made it a den of thieves. Have you never read that out of the mouths of babes and suckling's I have perfected praise?

****

Faith in Christ

He curses the fig tree for having no fruit, and says to it; Let no fruit grow on thee from this day until forever.

Truly I say to you, that if you shall have faith and doubt not, you shall not only do what is done to this fig tree, but also if you shall say to this mountain, be thou removed and be thou cast into the sea; it shall be done.

And all things, whatever you shall ask in prayer, believing, you shall receive.

When asked by what authority he does these things he replied. I will also ask you a question, which if you will answer I will also tell you by what authority I do these things.

The baptism of John where was it from; Was it from heaven or of men? They would not tell him.

Then Jesus said; Neither by what authority by which I do these things will I tell you.

But what do you think? A certain man had two sons, and he came to the first and said; Son go to work today in my vineyard.

He said to him I will not; but afterward repented and he went. And he came to the second and said likewise, and he said yes I will go, but he really did not.

Which of the two did the will of his father? They said, the first. Then Jesus said, Truly I say to you that the publicans and the whores shall enter the kingdom of heaven before you.

For John came to you in the way of righteousness and you believed him not; but the publicans and the whores believed him; and you when you had seen this repented not afterward and believed him not.

Hear another parable; There was a certain householder which planted a vineyard and hedged it about, and dug a winepress in the middle of it, and built a tower, and lent it out to caretakers and went into a far country.

And when the time of the fruits harvest drew near, he sent his servants to the caretakers that they might receive the fruits of the vineyard.

And the caretakers took his servants and beat one, killed another and stoned the third.

Again he sent more servants than the first time and they did likewise to them also. But last of all he sent his son saying, surely they shall reverence him.

But when the caretakers saw the son, they said among themselves; this is the heir, come let us kill him and let us seize his inheritance.

And they caught him and threw him out of the vineyard and they slew him. When therefore the lord of that vineyard comes, what shall he do to those caretakers?

Did you never read the scriptures, The stone which the builders rejected, the same has become the head of the corner; this is the Lord's doing and it is marvelous in our eyes.

Therefore I say to you that the kingdom of God shall be taken from you, and be given to a nation bringing forth the fruits thereof.

And whoever shall fall on this stone shall be broken; but on whomever it shall fall, it will grind him to powder.

My Prayer….. Lord may I draw ever nearer to you in both word and in deed. That in that great and mighty day of your coming, I may be found worthy of your Kingdom… Amen

****

The Kings Sons Marriage

The kingdom of heaven is like a certain king which made a marriage for his son. And sent forth his servants to call them that were bidden to the wedding but they would not come.

Again he sent forth other servants, saying, Tell them which are bidden, behold I have prepared my dinner, my oxen and my fatlings are killed, and all things are ready, come to the marriage.

But they made light of it and went there own ways. One to his farm, another to his merchandise. And the remnant treated his servants spitefully and slew them.

But when the king heard this he was angry, and sent forth his armies, and destroyed those murderers and burnt up their city.

Then said he to his servants, the wedding is ready but those who were bidden were not worthy. Go you therefore into the highways, and as many as you shall find bid to the wedding.

So those servants went out into the highways, and bid as many as they found both bad and good; and the wedding was furnished with guests.

And when the king came in to see the guests, he saw a man there which had not on a wedding garment. And he said to him; Friend how did you come in here not wearing a wedding garment?

And he was speechless. Then said the king to his servants, bind him hand and foot, and take him away and cast him into outer darkness; there shall be weeping and gnashing of teeth.

For many are called but few are chosen.

****

Taxes

They tempted him asking if it was lawful to give tribute to Caesar or not? Jesus said, Why do you tempt me you hypocrites?

Pointing to the coin he said; Whose image and superscription is this? They said to him, Caesars. Render therefore unto Caesar the things which are Caesars, and unto God the things which are God's.

****

Foolish Questions

You do err not knowing the scriptures, nor the power of God. For in the resurrection they neither marry nor are they given in marriage but are like the angels of God in heaven.

But as touching the resurrection of the dead, have you not read that which was spoken to you by God; I am the God of Abraham, and the God of Isaac, and the God of Jacob.

God is not the God of the dead but of the living.

****

The Greatest Commandment

You shall love the Lord thy God, with all thy heart, with all thy mind, and with all thy soul. This is the first and the greatest commandment.

And the second is liken to it; you shall love thy neighbor as thy self. On these two commandments hang all the law and the prophets.

What do you think of Christ, who's Son is he? They said, the son of David.

Jesus said, How then does David in spirit call him Lord saying, The Lord said to my Lord, sit thou on my right hand until I make your enemies your footstool?

If David then calls him Lord, how then is he his son?

****

Religious Leaders are Rebuked

The scribes and the Pharisees sit in Moses seat, All therefore that they bid you to do, that observe and do; but do not the works which they do, for they say and do not.

For they bind heavy burdens which are grievous to be borne, and lay them on mens shoulders; but they themselves will not move them with one of their fingers.

But all their works they do to be seen of men; they make broad their phylacteries, and enlarge the borders of their garments.

And they love the uppermost rooms at feasts, and the chief seats in the synagogues. And greetings in the market place to be called of men, Rabbi, Rabbi.

But be not called Rabbi, for one is your master, even Christ, and all you are brethren. And call no man father on earth, for one is your Father, and that is God in heaven.

Neither be called master, for one is your master, even Christ. But he that is greatest among you shall be your servant.

And whoever shall exalt himself shall be abased, and he that shall humble himself, shall be exalted.

But woe to you, scribes and Pharisses, hypocrites!

For you devour widow's houses, and for a pretense make long prayers, therefore you shall receive the greater damnation.

But woe to you! Scribes and Pharisees, hypocrites, for you encompass sea and land to make one proselyte, and when he is made, you make him twofold the child of hell that you are.

Woe unto you, you blind guides which say, whoever shall swear by the temple it is nothing; but whoever shall swear by the gold of the temple, he is a debtor!

You are fools and blind; for which is greater the gold or the temple which sanctifies the gold?

And whoever shall swear by the altar, it is nothing; but whoever shall swear by the gift that is on it, he is guilty.

You are fools and blind, for which is greater, the gift or the altar which sanctifies the gift?

Whoever therefore swears by the altar, swears by it and all the things on it. And whoever swears by the temple, swears by it, and by him that dwells therein.

And he that shall swear by heaven, swears by the throne of God and by him that sits thereon. Woe to you scribes and Pharisees, hypocrites!

For you pay a tithe of mint and anise and cumin, and have omitted the weightier matters of the law, judgment, mercy, and faith; these you should have done and not to leave the others undone.

You are blind guides, which strain at a gnat, and swallow a camel. Woe to you scribes and Pharissees, hypocrites!

For you make clean the outside of the cup and of the platter, but within they are full of extortion and excess.

You blind Pharisee, cleanse first that which is within the cup and platter that the outside of them may be clean also. Woe to you scribes and Pharisees, hypocrites!

For you are like a tomb painted white, which indeed appears beautiful on the outside, but within is full of dead mens bones and all uncleanliness.

Even so you also appear righteous outwardly to men, but within you are full of hypocrisy and iniquity.

Woe to you scribes and Pharisees, hypocrites! Because you build the tombs of the prophets, and garnish the graves of the righteousness.

And say, If we had been in the day of our fathers, we would have not been partakers with them in the blood of the prophets.

Therefore you are witnesses to yourselves that you are the children of them which killed the prophets. Fill you up then the measure of your fathers.

You serpents, you generation of vipers, how can you escape the damnation of hell?

Wherefore I send unto you prophets, and wise men and scribes; and some of them you shall kill and crucify; and some of them you scourge in your synagogues, and persecute them from city to city.

That upon you may come all the righteous blood shed upon the whole earth, from the blood of righteous Abel unto the blood of Zachariah son of Barachias, whom you killed between the temple and the altar.

Truly I say to you, all these things shall come upon this generation.

Oh Jerusalem, Jerusalem, you that kill the prophets and stone them which are sent to you.

How often would I have gathered your children together, even as a hen gathers her chicks together under her wings, and you would not have me.

Behold your house is left desolate. For I say to you, you shall not see me from this day, until you shall say, blessed is he who comes in the name of the Lord.

My prayer ….. May I never esteem myself Lord more highly than I should. Help me to be humble in your sight, and may I grow in your love towards my own neighbors day by day… Amen

****

Certain Destruction Foretold

Do you see all these things? Truly I say to you, there shall not be left one stone upon another that shall not be thrown down. Take heed that no man deceive you.

For many shall come in my name and shall say, I am Christ, and shall deceive many. And you shall hear of wars and rumors of wars; see that you be not troubled, but the end is not yet.

For nation shall rise against nation, and kingdom against kingdom; there shall be famines and pestilences and earthquakes in many places.

All of these are the beginnings of sorrows.

Then they shall deliver you up to be afflicted and shall kill you; and you shall be hated of all nations for my namesake.

And then shall many be offended, and shall betray one another, and shall hate one another. And many false prophets shall arise and shall deceive many.

And because iniquity shall abound the love of many shall wax cold. But he that endures to the end, the same shall be saved.

And this gospel of the kingdom shall be preached in all the world for a witness to all nations; and then shall the end come.

When you then shall see the abomination of desolation, spoken by Daniel the prophet, stand in the holy place, then let them which be in Judea flee into the mountains.

Let him who is on the housetop not come down to take anything out of his house. Neither let him that is in the field return back to get his clothes.

And woe to them that are with child and to them that give suck in those days. But pray then that your flight be not in winter or on the sabbath day.

For then shall be great tribulation, such as was not since the beginning of the world to this time, nor ever shall be.

And except those days be shortened, there should no flesh be saved; but for the elects sake those days shall be shortened.

Then if any man should say to you, here is the Christ, or here, believe them not.

For there shall arise false Christ's and false prophets, and shall show great wonders and signs, in as much if were possible they shall deceive the very elect.

Behold, I have told you before. Wherefore if they shall say to you, behold he is in the desert; go not there; behold he is in secret chambers; believe it not.

For as lightening comes out of the east and shines into the west; so shall also the coming of the Son of man be.

For wherever the carcass lies there shall the eagles be gathered together.

Immediately after the tribulation of those days shall the sun be darkened, and the moon shall not give her light, and the stars shall fall from heaven, and the powers of the heavens shall be shaken.

And then shall appear the sign of the Son of man in heaven, and then shall all the tribes of the earth mourn.

And they shall see the Son of man in the clouds coming with power and great glory.

And he shall send his angels with a great sound of a trumpet, and they shall gather together his elect from the four winds, from one end of heaven to the other.

Now learn a parable of the fig tree; When his branch is yet tender he puts forth leaves, you know that summer is near.

So likewise you, when you shall see all these things, know that it is near, even at the door.

Truly I say to you this generation shall not pass until all these things be fulfilled. Heaven and earthy shall pass away, but my words shall never pass away.

But of that day and hour knows no man, not even the angels in heaven, but my Father only. But as it was in the days of Noah, so shall it be also at the coming of the Son of man.

For as in the days before the flood they were eating and drinking, marrying and giving in marriage, until the day that Noah entered into the ark.

And they knew not until the flood came and took them all away; so shall the coming of the Son of man be. Then two shall be in the field, one shall be taken and the other shall be left.

Two women shall be grinding at the mill, one shall be taken and the other shall be left. Watch therefore for you know not what hour your Lord comes.

But know this, that if the goodman of the house had known at what hour the thief would come, he would have watched and not allowed his house to be broken into.

Therefore you also be ready, for in such an hour as you think not, the Son of man shall come. Who then is a faithful and wise servant, whom his lord has made ruler over his household, to give them meat in due season?

Blessed is that servant, whom his lord when he comes shall find him so doing. Truly I say to you that he shall make him ruler over all his goods.

But and if that evil servant shall say in his heart, my Lord delays his coming; and shall begin to smite his fellow servants, and to eat and drink with the drunken.

The lord of that servant shall come in a day when he is not looking for him, and in an hour that he is not aware of.

And shall cut him in two, and appoint him his portion among the hypocrites; there shall be weeping and gnashing of teeth.

My Prayer….. Lord may I be counted among the blessed in that wondrous day. Use me as a faithful witness of your love and your greatness… Amen

****

Christ is Conspired Against

You know that after two days is the feast of the Passover, and the Son of man is betrayed to be crucified.

After the woman had anointed Christ with costly oils and perfumes he said to those that were present, who were complaining that she was wasting expensive perfume, Why do you trouble the woman? For she has done a good work to me.

For you have the poor always with you, but me you have not always with you. For in that she has poured this ointment upon my body, she did it for my burial.

Truly I say unto you, that where ever this gospel shall be preached in this whole world, there shall also this, that this woman has done, be told for a memorial of her.

****

The Passover and Betrayal

Go into the city to such a man, and say unto him, the Master says my time is at hand; I will keep the Passover at your house with my disciples.

Truly I say to you that one of you shall betray me. He that dips his hand with me into the dish, the same shall betray me.

The Son of Man goes as it is written of him; but woe unto that man by whom the Son of Man is betrayed! It had been good for that man if he had not been born.

Take and eat; this is my body. Drink you all of it; for this is my blood of the new testament, which is shed for many for the remission of sins.

But I say to you, I will not drink from this time, of this fruit of the vine, until I drink it new with you in my Fathers kingdom.

All of you shall be offended because of me this night; for it is written; I will smite the Shepard and the sheep of the flock shall be scattered abroad.

But after I am risen again, I will go before you into Galilee. Peter then said to him; I will never deny you.

After Peter said this, Jesus said, truly I say to you, that this night before the cock crows, you shall deny me three times.

Sit here while I go and pray over yonder. He took with him Peter and the two sons of Zebedee.

He said to them; My soul is exceedingly sorrowful, even unto death; tarry you here and wait with me.

Oh my Father if it be possible let this cup pass from me; nevertheless not as I will but as you will.

He came to the disciples and they were asleep. He said to them; Could you not watch with me for one hour?

Watch and pray that you enter not into temptation; the spirit is indeed willing but the flesh is weak.

Oh my Father if this cup may not pass away from me, except I drink of it, thy will be done.

Sleep on now, and take your rest; Behold, the hour is at hand, and the Son of man is betrayed into the hands of sinners. Rise, let us be going, he is at hand that does betray me.

After Judas kissed him he said; Friend wherefore have you come? Then Peter slashed one of the soldier's ears off.

Put up your sword into its place, For he that lives by the sword shall die by the sword. Do you think that I cannot even now pray to my Father, and he shall immediately send me more than twelve legions of angels?

But how then shall the scriptures be fulfilled that thus it must be? Have you come out as against a thief with swords and staves to take me?

I sat daily with you teaching in the temple, and you took no hold on me. But this was done that the scriptures of the prophets might be fulfilled.

****

False Witnesses Testify

Two false witnesses came and said to Pilate; This fellow said that he would destroy the temple of God and that he would rebuild it in three days. Then Pilate said to Jesus; What do you have to say to this? Jesus remained silent. Pilate then said; I adjure you, are you the Son of God? Jesus said; You have said so; Nevertheless I say to you that hereafter you shall see the Son of man sitting on the right hand of power, and coming in the clouds of heaven.

****

After the Resurrection

After the crucifixion he appeared to some of the disciples saying; All Hail, Be not afraid; go tell my brethren, that they should go into Galilee and there I shall see them. Later on he did come to them and said; All power is given to me in heaven and on earth.

You go therefore and teach all nations, baptizing them in the name of the Father, and of the Son, and of the Holy Ghost.

Teaching them to observe all the things which I commanded you; and lo I am with you always, even to the end of the world.

My prayer….. Lord as you remained faithful, trusting in your Father until death. May I also remain a faithful servant to the end. Until that time when I shall see you and the saints of God in heaven… Amen

From the Gospel of Saint Mark

The Apostles are Called

The time is fulfilled, and the kingdom of God is at hand, repent and believe in the gospel. Come after me and I will make you to become fishers of men.

Let us go into the next towns, that there I may preach also; for therefore came I forth.

****

The Leper Healed

A certain leper shouted to him; Master have mercy on me. He said to him; What will you have me to do for you. The man said; That I might be healed. Jesus said to him; I will; be thou clean. See that you say nothing to any man; but go your way; show yourself to the priest, and offer for your cleansing those things which Moses commanded for a testimony to them.

****

Persistent Faith

He said to a sick man; Son your sins be forgiven you, and he was immediately made well .The scribes then said among themselves; Who is he to forgive sins? To the scribes he said; Why reason you these things in your heart?

For is it easier to say to the one sick of the palsy, your sins are forgiven you, or to say, arise, take up your bed and walk?

But that you may know that the Son of man has power on earth to forgive sins, I say to you, arise, take up your bed and go into your house.

They that are whole have no need for a physician, but they that are sick; I came not to call the righteous but sinners to repentance.

Can the children of the bride chamber fast, while the bridegroom is with them? As long as they have the bridegroom with them they cannot fast.

But the days will come when the bridegroom shall be taken away from them, and then they shall fast in those days.

No man also sews a piece of new cloth into an old garment; or else the new piece that filled it up, takes away from the old and the tear is made worse.

And no man puts new wine in old bottles; or else the new wine does burst the bottles, and the wine is spilled out, and the bottles will be marred.

But new wine must be put into new bottles.

Have you never read what David did, when he had need, and was hungry, him and those who were with him?

How he went into the house of God in the days of Abiathar the high priest, and did eat the showbread, which is not lawful to eat except for the priests, and gave also to them which were with him?

The Sabbath was made for man, and not man for the Sabbath.

How can Satan cast out Satan? And if a kingdom be divided against itself, that kingdom cannot stand.

And if Satan rises up against himself, and is divided, he cannot stand, but has an end.

No man can enter into a strong mans house, and spoil his goods, except he will first bind the strong man, and then he will spoil his house.

Truly I say to you, all sins shall be forgiven the sons of men, and blasphemies wherewith they shall blaspheme.

But he that shall blaspheme against the Holy Ghost has never forgiveness, but is in danger of eternal damnation.

Who is my mother, or my brethren? Behold my mother and my brethren! For whoever shall do the will of my Father, the same is my mother, my brother, and my sister.

****

The Parable of the Sower

Hearken; Behold a sower went out to sow; and it came to pass as he sowed that some fell by the way side, and the fowls of the air came and devoured it up.

And some fell on stony ground, where it had not much earth, and immediately it sprung up because it had not much earth.

But when the sun came up it was scorched because it had not much earth and it withered away.

And some fell among thorns, and the thorns grew up and choked it out, and it yielded no fruit.

And other fell on good ground, and did yield fruit that sprang up and increased; and brought forth some thirty, some sixty and some one hundredfold. He that has ears let him hear.

Unto you it is given to know the mystery of the kingdom of God; but unto them that are without these things are done in parables; that seeing they may see and not perceive; and hearing they may hear and not understand; lest at any time they should be converted and their sins be forgiven them.

Know you not his parable? And how then will you know all parables?

The sower sows the word; and these are they by the wayside, where the word is sown; but when they have heard, Satan comes immediately, and takes away the word that was sown in their hearts.

And these are they likewise which are sown on stony ground; who, when they have heard the word, immediately receive it with gladness; and have no root in themselves.

And so they endure but for a time; and afterward when affliction or persecution arises for the words sake, immediately they are offended.

And these are they which are sown among thorns; such as hear the word of God, and the cares of this world, and the deceitfulness of riches, and the lusts of other things enter in, choke the word, and it becomes unfruitful.

And these are they which are sown on good ground; such as hear the word, and receive it, and bring forth fruit, some thirty, some sixty, and some one hundredfold.

Is a candle brought to be hid under a bushel basket, or under a bed? And not rather to be put on a candlestick?

For there is nothing hid that shall not be manifested; neither was anything kept secret, but that it should come abroad.

If any man has ears to hear, let him hear. Take heed what you hear, with whatever measure you measure, it shall be measured unto you; and to you that hear more shall be given.

For he that has to him shall be given more; and him that has not; from him shall be taken even that which he has.

So is the kingdom of God, as if a man should cast seed into the ground; And should sleep, and the seed should spring up and grow, he knows not how.

For the earth brings forth fruit of herself; first the blade, then the ear, after that the full ear of corn.

But when the fruit is brought forth, immediately he puts in the sickle for the harvest has come. Whereunto shall we compare the kingdom of God?

Or with what comparison shall we compare it? It is like a grain of mustard seed, which when it is sown in the earth, is less than all seeds that are put into the earth in size.

But when it is sown it grows up, and becomes greater than all the herbs, and shoots out great branches; so that all the fowls in the air can lodge under the shadow of it.

My prayer….. May my life be as that fertile ground, and bring forth much fruit into your kingdom Lord Jesus…Amen

****

The Man Delivered of Many Devils

Christ after having rebuked the devils that had held a man captive for many years said to him; Go home to your friends, and tell them how great things the Lord has done for you, and has had compassion on you.

****

The Woman with the Issue of Blood

While walking with his disciples through a crowd of people who were pressing against him and trying to touch him, Jesus said; Who touched my clothes? His disciples said; How can we tell who touched you with so many people pressing hard against us? With that a woman in fear fell down before him. He said to her; Daughter your faith has made you whole; go in peace and be made whole of your plague.

****

Jairus Daughter is Raised

Be not afraid but only believe. Why make you this big to do and weep? The damsel is not dead, but sleeping.

He said to her; Talitha cumi, which being interpreted is, damsel I say unto you arise, and she rose from the dead and walked about.

****

Christ's Rejection and the Twelve Sent Forth

A prophet is not without honor, but in his own country, and among his own kin, and in his own house. In whatsoever place, you shall enter into a house, there abide until; you depart from that place.

And whosoever shall not receive you, nor hear you, when you depart from there, shake off the dust under your feet for a testimony against them.

Truly I say to you, it shall be more tolerable for Sodom and Gomorrah in the day of judgment, than for that city.

****

Traditions Rebuked and Dishonoring God's Word

Well has Isaiah prophesied of you hypocrites, as it is written, these people honor me with their lips, but their heart is far from me.

Howbeit in vain they do worship me, teaching for doctrines the commandments of men.

For laying aside the commandments of God, you hold on to the traditions of men, like the washing of pots and cups; and many other such things as that you do.

Full well you reject the commandment of God, that you may keep your traditions. For Moses said, honor thy father and thy mother; and whosoever curses father or mother let him die the death.

But you say, if a man shall say to his father or mother, it is Corban, that is to say, a gift, by whatsoever you may be profited by me; he shall be free.

And you suffer him no more to do anything for his father or mother; making the word of God of no effect, through your tradition which you have delivered; and many such things as these you do.

Listen unto me every one of you, and understand. There is nothing from outside of a man, that entering into the man can defile him; but the things which come out of him, these are the things which defile him. If any man has ears to hear let him hear.

****

Jesus Expounds Upon the Parable

Are you without understanding also? Do you not perceive that anything from without a man cannot defile him by entering into him?

Because it enters not into his heart, but into his belly, and goes out into the draught, purging all meats? That which comes out of the man, defiles the man.

For from within, out of the heart of man, proceeds evil thoughts, adulteries, fornications, and murders.

Thefts, covetousness, wickedness, deceit, lasciviousness, an evil eye, blasphemy, pride and foolishness. All these evil things come from within and defile the man.

****

The Syrophenician Woman's Daughter is Healed

Let the children first be filled; for it is not meet to take the children's bread, and cast it to the dogs.

The woman said to him, Yes Lord; yet even the dogs under the table eat the children's crumbs.

He said to her; For this saying go your way; the devil is gone out of your daughter.

****

Four Thousand are Fed

I have compassion on the multitude, because they have been with me now three days and have nothing to eat.

And if I send them away fasting to their own houses, they will faint in the way; for many of them came from far away. How many loves do you have?

Christ took the seven loaves and blessed them and fed them all.

****

Sign Seekers Rebuked

Why does this generation seek after a sign? Truly I say unto you there shall no sign be given unto this generation.

Take heed; beware of the leaven of the Pharisees, and of the leaven of Herod.

Why reason you because you have no bread? Do you not yet perceive nor yet understand? Have you your heart hardened? Having eyes you see not?

And having ears you hear not? And do you not remember? When I broke the five loaves among five thousand, how many baskets you had left?

And when I broke the seven among the four thousand, how many baskets you picked up? How is it that you do not understand?

****

Christ's Rebuke of Peter

Get the behind me Satan; for you savor not the things that be of God, but the things that be of men.

Whoever will come after me, let him deny himself, pick up his cross and follow me.

For whoever will save his life shall lose it; but whoever shall lose his life for my sake and the gospels; the same shall save it.

For what shall it profit a man if he shall gain the whole world and lose his soul?

Or what shall a man give in exchange for his soul?

Whoever therefore shall be ashamed of me and of my words in this adulterous and sinful generation; of him also shall the Son of man be ashamed, when he comes in the glory of his Father with the holy angels.

Truly I say unto you, that there be some of them standing here with me, which shall not taste death, till they have seen the kingdom of God come with great power.

Elijah truly came first and restored all things; and how it is written of the Son of man, that he must suffer many things and be set at naught.

But I say to you, that Elijah has indeed come, and they have done with him whatever they wanted, as it is written of him.

****

The Healing of the Demoniac Son

What question you with him faithless generation, how long shall I be with you? How long shall I suffer you? Bring him to me.

How long ago is it since this came upon him? If you can believe, all things are possible to him that believes.

You dumb and deaf spirit, I charge you to come out of him, and to enter not into him again. This kind comes out by nothing except by prayer and fasting.

****

His Death Foretold and Their Ambitions Rebuked

The Son of man is delivered into the hands of men, and they shall kill him; and after that he is killed he shall rise the third day.

What was it that you disputed among yourselves by the way? If any man desires to be first, the same shall be last of all and servant of all.

He took a child to himself and said Whosoever shall receive one of such children in my name, receives me; and whoever receives me, receives not me, but him who sent me.

****

The Apostles Question and Casting out Devils

Forbid him not; for there is no man which shall do a miracle in my name that can lightly speak evil of me. For he that is not against us is for us.

For whoever shall give you a cup of water to drink in my name, because you belong to Christ, truly I say unto you, he shall in no wise lose his reward.

And whosoever shall offend one of these little ones that believes in me, it is better for him that a millstone should be hanged around his neck, and he were cast into the sea.

And if your hand offend you, cut it off; it is better for you to enter into life maimed, than having two hands and go into hell, into the fire that shall never be quenched.

Where their worm dieth not, and the fire is never quenched. For everyone shall be salted with fire, and every sacrifice shall be salted with salt.

Salt is good; but if the salt has lost his saltiness, with what shall you season it? Have salt in yourselves, and have peace with one another.

My Prayer….. Help me this day Lord to use the faith which you have given to me… Amen

****

Marriage and its Sacredness

What did Moses command you? For the hardness of your heart he wrote you this precept. But from the beginning of creation God made them male and female.
For this cause shall a man leave his father and mother and cleave to his wife. And the two shall be one flesh; so they are no more two but one.

What therefore God has put together let no man put asunder.

Whosoever shall put away his wife and marry another, commits adultery against her. And if a woman shall put away her husband and marry another, she commits adultery.

****

Little Children

Suffer the little children to come to me, and forbid them not; for of such is the kingdom of God.

Truly I say unto you, whoever shall not receive the kingdom of God as a little child, shall in no way enter therein.

****

Riches Perils

Why do you call me good? There is none good but one, that is God.

You know the commandments, do not commit adultery, do not kill, do not bear false witness, defraud not, honor thy mother and father.

To the rich ruler he then said; One thing you lack; go your way and sell whatever you have and give to the poor, and you shall have treasure in heaven; and come, take up your cross and follow me.

How hardly shall they that have riches enter into the kingdom of God! Children, how hard is it for them that trust in riches to enter into the kingdom of God!

It is easier for a camel to go through the eye of a needle than for a rich man to enter into the kingdom of God. With men it is impossible, but not with God; for with God all things are possible.

Truly I say to you, there is no man that has left house, or bretheren, or sisters, or brothers, or father, or mother, or wife, or children, or lands, for my sake, and the gospels.

But he shall receive a hundredfold now in this time, houses, and brethren, and sisters, and mothers, and children, and lands, with persecutions; and in the world to come, eternal life.

But many that are first shall be last, and the last, first.

****

Christ Foretells His Death and James and Johns Debate

Behold we go up to Jerusalem; and the Son of man shall be delivered to the chief priests and to the scribes; and they shall condemn him to death, and shall deliver him to the Gentiles.

And they shall mock him, and shall scourge him, and shall spit upon him, and shall kill him, and on the third day he shall rise again.

In response to James and John he said; what would you have me to do for you? You know not what you ask; can you drink of the cup that I drink of? And be baptized with the baptism that I am baptized with?

They said yes. He said to them; You shall indeed drink of the cup that I drink of; and be baptized with the baptism that I am baptized with.

But to sit on my right hand and on my left is not mine to give; but it shall be given to them for whom it is prepared.

You know that they which are accounted to rule over the Gentiles exercise lordship over them; and their great ones exercise authority over them.

But so shall it not be among you; but whoever will be great among you, shall be your minister; and whoever among you that shall be chief, shall be servant of all.

For even the Son of man came not to be ministered to, but to minister, and to give his life a ransom for many.

****

Blind Bartimaeus Healed

What will you that I should do for you? He said to Christ; That I might see. Jesus said; Go your way; your faith has made you whole.

****

The Triumphant Entry into Jerusalem

Go your way into the village over against you; and as soon as you have entered into it, you will find a colt tied whereon a man has never sat; loose him and bring him to me.

And if any man says unto you, why do you do this? Just say that the Lord has need of him; and straightway he will send him here.

****

The Temple Cleansing

Is it not written, my house shall be called of all nations, a house of prayer? But you have made it a den of thieves.

****

The Fig Tree Withers

Peter then in amazement says, Master the fig tree withered away. Jesus said. Have faith in God.

For truly I say unto you, that whoever shall say to this mountain, be thou removed, and be thou cast into the sea.

And shall not doubt in his heart, but shall believe that those things which he said shall come to pass; he shall have whatever he says.

Therefore I say unto you whatsoever things you desire when you pray, believe that you receive them and you shall have them.

And when you stand praying, forgive, if you have anything against anybody; that your Father which is in heaven may forgive your trespasses.

But if you do not forgive, neither will your Father which is in heaven forgive your trespasses.

****

His Authority is Challenged

I will also ask you a question, and answer me, and I will tell you by what authority I do these things. The baptism of John, was it from heaven or of men? Answer me.

This was said in response to the religious leaders questioning his authority.

They would not answer his question about the baptism of John, whether it was of men or of God.

He then said; Neither do I tell you by what authority I do these things.

****

Parable of the Evil Husbandmen

A certain man planted a vineyard, and set a hedge about it, and dug a place for the wine fat, and built a tower, and let it out to husbandmen and went into a far country.

And at the season he sent to the husbandmen a servant that he might receive from the husbandmen of the fruit of the vineyard.

And they caught him, and beat him, and sent him away empty.

And again he sent to them another servant; and at him they cast stones, wounding him in the head, and sent him away shamefully handled.

And again he sent another, and him they killed; and many others; beating some and killing some.

Having therefore one son, his well beloved, he sent him also last to them, saying, they will reverence my son.

But those husbandmen said amongst themselves, this is the heir, come lets kill him, and the inheritance shall be ours. And they took him and killed him and cast him out of the vineyard.

What shall therefore the lord of the vineyard do? He will come and destroy the husbandmen and give the vineyard to others.

And have you not read this scripture; The stone which the builders rejected is become the corner stone?

This was the Lord's doing and it is marvelous in our eyes.

****

The Question of Caesars Tribute

Why do you tempt me? Bring me a penny, that I might see it. Whose is this image and whose superscription is it?

Render to Caesar therefore the things that are Caesars, and to God the things that are God's.

The Sadducees were silenced. He continued saying; Do you not therefore err, because you know not the scriptures, neither the power of God?

For when they shall rise from the dead, they neither marry nor are they given in marriage, but are as the angels which are in heaven.

And as touching the dead, that they rise; have you not read in the book of Moses, how in the bush God spoke to him, saying, I am the God of Abraham, and the God of Isaac, and the God of Jacob?

He is not therefore the God of the dead, but of the living; you therefore do greatly err.

****

The Greatest Commandment

The first of all the commandments is, Hear oh Israel; The Lord our God is one Lord.

And thou shall love the Lord thy God with all your heart, and with all your soul, and with all your mind, and with all your strength; this is the first commandment.

And the second is namely this, You shall love your neighbor as yourself. There is no other commandment greater than these.

****

A Scribe is Commended

You are not far from the kingdom of God. How say the scribes that Christ is the son of David?

For David him self said by the Holy Ghost, The Lord said to my Lord, sit thou on my right hand, until; I make your enemies your footstool.

David therefore himself calls him Lord; so how can he be his son?

Beware of the scribes which love to go about in long clothing, and love salutations in the marketplaces, and the chief seats in the synagogues, and the uppermost rooms at feasts.

Which devour widow's houses, and for pretence make long prayers; these shall receive greater damnation.

****

The Widows Mite

Truly I say to you, That this poor widow has cast more in then all those who have cast money into the treasury.

For they all did cast in out of their abundance; but she out of her want did cast in all that she had, even all of her living.

My Prayer….. Help us Lord to love you with all that is within us. And that I would never think more highly of myself then I should… Amen

****

Christ Tells of the Future

Do you see these great buildings? There shall not be left one stone upon another that shall not be thrown down.

Take heed that no man may deceive you. For many shall come in my name and say I am Christ; and shall deceive many.

And when you shall hear of wars and rumors of wars, be not troubled for such things must need be; but the end shall not be yet.

For nation shall rise against nation, and kingdom against kingdom; and there shall be earthquakes in divers places, and there shall be famines and troubles; these are the beginnings of sorrows.

But take heed to yourselves; for they shall deliver you up to councils; and in the synagogues you shall be beaten.

And you shall be brought before rulers and kings for my names sake, and for a testimony against them.

And the gospel must first be published among all nations. But when they shall lead you and deliver you up, take no thought before hand what you shall speak, neither should you pre meditate.

Whatever shall be given to you in that hour, that you should speak, for it is not you that speak but the Holy Ghost.

Now the brother shall betray the brother to death; and the father the son; and the children shall rise up against their parents, and shall cause them to be put to death.

And you shall be hated of all men for my name sake; but he that shall endure to the end the same shall be saved.

But when you shall see the abomination of desolation, spoken of by Daniel the prophet, standing where it ought not, (let him that reads understand), then let them that be in Judea flee to the mountains.

And let him that is on the housetops not go down into the house, neither enter into it to take anything out of his house. And let him that is in the field not turn back again to pick up his garment.

But woe to them that are with child and to them that give suck in those days! And pray that your flight be not in winter.

For in those days shall be affliction such as was not from the beginning of the creation. Which God created until this time, neither shall be again.

And except that the Lord had shortened those days, no flesh would be saved; but for the elect's sake, whom he has chosen, he has shortened those days.

And if any man shall say to you, look here is the Christ; or look, he is over there; believe him not.

For false Christ's and false prophets shall arise, and shall show signs and wonders, to seduce if it were possible the very elect.

But take heed, behold I have told you all things. But in those days, after the tribulation, the son shall be darkened, and the moon shall not give her light.

And the stars of heaven shall fall, and that powers that be in heaven shall be shaken.

And then shall they see the Son of man coming in the clouds with great power and glory.

And he shall send his angels and gather together his elect, from the four winds, and from the uttermost parts of the earth to the uttermost part of heaven.

Now learn a parable of the fig tree; when her branch is yet tender, and puts forth leaves, you know that summer is near.

So you in like manner, when you shall see these things cone to pass, know that it is near even at the door.

Truly I say to you, that this generation shall not pass away until all these things have happened. Heaven and earth shall pass away but my words shall never pass away.

But of that day and hour knows no man, no, not even the angels of heaven, neither the Son, but the Father only.

Take heed, watch and pray; for you know not when the time is.

For the Son of man is as a man taking a far journey, who left his house, and gave authority to his servants, and to every man in his work, and commanded the porter to watch.

Watch you therefore, for you know not when the master of the house shall come, at even or at midnight, or when the cock crows in the morning.

Unless coming suddenly he finds you sleeping. And what I say to you I say to all, Watch.

****

The Bethany Anointing

Leave her alone, Why do you trouble her? she has wrought a good work for me.

For you have the poor with you always, whenever you will you may do good work to them; but me you have not always.

She has done what she could; she has come beforehand to anoint my body for the burial.

Truly I say to you, that wherever this gospel shall be preached throughout the whole world, this also that she has done shall be spoken of as a memorial to her.

****

The Passover

Go into the city and there you shall meet a man bearing a pitcher of water; follow him.

And wherever he shall go into, say to the goodman of the house, The Master says, where is the guestchamber where I shall eat the Passover with my disciples?

And he will show you a large upper room furnished and prepared; there make ready for us.

And in the evening they gathered there, Jesus said, Truly I say to you, one of you which eats with me shall betray me.

It is the one that dips with me into the dish. The Son of man indeed goes as it is written of him; but woe to that man by whom he is betrayed! Good were it for that man if he had never been born.

Take and eat, this is my body. This is my blood of the new testament which is shed for many.

Truly I say to you, I will drink no more of the fruit of the vine, until that day that I drink it new in the kingdom of God.

All of you shall be not offended because of me this night; for it is written, I will smite the Shepard and the sheep of the flock will be scattered.

But after I have risen I will go before you into Galilee. Truly I say unto you that this day, even this night, before the cock crows two times you shall deny me three times.

Sit here while I pray. My soul is exceedingly sorrowful even unto death; tarry you here and watch.

Abba, Father, all things are possible for you; take away this cup from me; nevertheless, not what I will but what you will.

Simon! Why do you sleep? Could you not watch for one hour? Watch and pray unless you enter into temptation. The spirit truly is ready but the flesh is weak.

He left and when he returned he found them asleep again. Sleep on now and take your rest; it is enough, the hour has come; behold the Son of man is betrayed into the hands of sinners.

Rise up let us go; he that betrays me is at hand.

Have you come out as against a thief, with swords and with staves to take me? I was daily with you in the temple teaching, and you took me not; but the scriptures must be fulfilled.

They took him into custody and later he was asked; Are you the Christ, the Son of the Blessed?

I am and you shall see the Son of man sitting on the right hand of power, and coming in the clouds of heaven.

****

On the Cross

Eloi, Eloi, lama sabach thani. Which being interpreted means, My God, My God, why have you forsaken me? With that he gave up the ghost.

****

After His Resurrection

Go you into all the world, and preach the gospel to every creature. He that believes and is baptized shall be saved; but he that believes not shall be damned.

And these signs shall follow them that believe; in my name they shall cast out devils; they shall speak with new tongues.

They shall take up serpents; and if they drink any deadly thing, it shall not hurt them; and they shall lay hands on the sick and they shall recover.

****

From the Gospel of Saint Luke

Mary and Joseph find the young boy Jesus in the temple; Jesus said to them; How is it that you sought after me? Did you not know that I must be about my Fathers business?

****

His Responses to Satan

It is written, That man shall not live by bread alone, but by every word of God.

And then the second temptation is answered with; Get thee behind me Satan; for it is written, you shall worship the Lord thy God and him only shall you serve.

And yet a third temptation is answered; It is said, you shall not tempt the Lord thy God.

****

In the Synagogue on the Sabbath

The Spirit of the Lord is upon me, because he has anointed me to preach the gospel to the poor.

He sent me to heal the brokenhearted, to preach deliverance to the captives, and recovering of sight to the blind, to set at liberty them that are bruised.

To preach the acceptable year of the Lord. This day is this scripture fulfilled in your ears.

You will surely say to me this proverb, Physician, heal yourself; whatever we have heard that was done in Capernaum, do here also in your own country.

Truly I say to you that no prophet is accepted in his own country.

But I will tell you a truth, many widows were in Israel in the days of Elijah, when the heavens were shut up for three years and six months, when great famine was throughout all the land.

But to none of them was Elijah sent, except to Serepta, a city of Sidon, to a woman that was a widow.

And many lepers were in Israel in the time of Elisha the prophet; and none of them were cleansed, except Naaman the Syrian.

****

At Capernaum

To the demon possessed man he said, Hold your peace and come out of him. And later he said, I must preach the kingdom of God in other cities also; for this cause I have been sent.

****

By the Waterfront

Standing on the shore he shouted to the disciples in the boat; Launch out into the deep and let down your nets for a draught. Their nets were filled to the bursting!

Fear not for from this day forward you shall catch men.

****

The Leper

The leper fell on his face before Him and said, If you will you can make me clean, Jesus said to him; I will, be thou made clean.

Now go and tell no man; but go and show yourself to the priest and offer for your cleansing, according as Moses commanded, for a testimony to them.

Then later to a paralytic man He said; Man your sins are forgiven you. And he got up and walked.

****

The Ability to Forgive Sin

What do you reason in your hearts? Which is easier to say, thy sins be forgiven you or rise up and walk?

But that you may know that the Son of man has power on earth to forgive sins, I say to you, Arise, take up your couch, and go into your house.

After this he saw Matthew sitting at customs and said to him; Follow me!

They that are whole do not need a physician; but those that are sick. I came not to call the righteous but sinners to repentance.

The leaders asked him, why his disciples did not fast? He said, Can you make the children of the bride chamber fast while the groom is with them?

But the days will come, when the bridegroom shall be taken away from them, and then shall they fast in those days.

No man can put a piece of new garment into an old one, otherwise the new piece will make a tear and the old piece will not agree with the new one.

And no man puts new wine into old bottles, or else the new wine will burst the old bottles, and be spilled, and the bottles will perish.

But new wine must be put into new bottles and both will be preserved. No man also having drunk old wine immediately desires new; for he says the old is much better.

****

The Sabbath and the Withered Hand

Have you not read so much as this, what David did, when he and those that were with him did when they were hungry?

How he went into the house of God and did eat the showbread, and gave it also to them that were with him; which was not lawful to eat but for the priests alone.

The Son of man is Lord of the Sabbath also. With that a man rose up in the synagogue on the Sabbath whose hand was withered, Jesus said to him; Rise up, and stand forth in the midst of everyone.

Then Jesus said to them; I will ask you one thing; is it lawful on the Sabbath days to do good, or to do evil? To save life, or to destroy it?

He said to the man; Stretch forth your hand, and he was healed immediately.

****

The Sermon on the Plain

Blessed be the poor; for yours is the kingdom of God. Blessed are you that hunger now, for you shall be filled. Blessed are you that weep now, for you shall laugh.

Blessed are you when men shall hate you, and when they shall separate you from their company, and shall reproach you, and cast out your name as evil for the Son of mans sake.

Rejoice in that day and leap for joy; for behold your reward is great in heaven; for in like manner did their fathers to the prophets.

But woe unto you that are rich! For you have received your consolation. Woe unto you that are full!

For you shall hunger! Woe unto you that laugh now! For you shall mourn and weep. Woe unto you when all men shall speak well of you! For so did their fathers of the false prophets.

But I say to those who hear, love your enemies, and do good to them which hate you.

Bless them that curse you, and pray for them which despitefully use you. And to him that smites you on the one cheek offer also the other; and to him that takes your cloak, allow him also to take your coat.

Give to every man that asks of you; and from him that takes away your goods, ask for them not to be given back again. And as you would have men to do to you, do to them likewise also.

For if you love them that love you also, what thanks have you? For sinners also do the same.

And if you lend to them of whom you have hopes of receiving it again, what thanks have you? For sinners also lend to sinners, to receive as much again.

But love your enemies, and do good, and lend, hoping for nothing in return; and your reward shall be great, and you shall be the children of the Highest; for he is kind to the unthankful and to the evil.

Be you therefore merciful as your Father is merciful. Judge not and you shall not be judged; condemn not and you shall not be condemned; forgive and you shall be forgiven;

Give and it shall be given you; good measure, pressed down, and shaken together, and running over shall men give unto your bosom. For with the same measure with which you measure, it shall be measured to you again.

Can the blind lead the blind? Shall not both fall into the ditch? The disciple is not above his master; but everyone that is perfect shall be as his master.

And why do you behold the speck that is in your brothers eye; and you perceive not the beam that is in your own?

Neither can you say to your brother, Brother, let me pull out the speck that is in your eye, when you yourself cannot perceive the beam that is in your own eye?

You hypocrite! Cast out first the beam that is in your own eye, then you shall see clearly to remove the speck that is in your brothers eye.

For a good tree does not bring forth corrupt fruit; neither does a corrupt tree bring forth good fruit. For every tree is known by its own fruit.

For from thorns men do not gather figs, neither from a bramble bush do they gather grapes.

A good man out of the good treasure of his heart brings forth that which is good; and an evil man out of the evil treasure of his heart brings forth that which is evil; for out of the abundance of the heart the mouth speaks.

And why do you call me, Lord, Lord, and do not the things which I say? Whoever comes to me, and hears my sayings, and does them, I will show you who he is like.

He is like a man who built a house, and dug deep, and laid the foundation on a rock; and when the floods arose and the waters beat vehemently against the house, it could not shake it, for its foundation was built upon a rock.

But he that hears my words, and does not do them, is like a man that without a foundation built his house upon the earth; against which the water did beat vehemently; and immediately it fell; and the ruin of that house was great.

My Prayer.....Keep me close to you Lord, may I always listen to, and do those things which you say. Help me Lord to be the best Christian that I can be...Amen

****

Raising the Widows Son

Jesus sees a widows funeral procession with her only son in the bier, he says to her; Weep not, then he came and touched the bier and said; Young man, I say unto you, Arise! And he sat up and began to speak.

****

His Answer to John the Baptists Disciples

Go your way, and tell John what things you have both seen and heard; how the blind see, the lame walk, the lepers are cleansed, the deaf hear, the dead are raised and to the poor the gospel is preached.

And blessed is he whoever shall not be offended in me.

He then begins to talk to the disciples of John the bapstist. What did you go out into the wilderness to see?

A reed shaken in the wind? But what did you go out to see? A man clothed in soft clothing?

Behold they which are gorgeously appareled and live delicately, are in king's courts. But what did you go out to see? A prophet?

Yes I say to you and much more than a prophet.

This is he of whom it is written, behold I send my messenger before your face, which shall prepare your way before you.

For I say unto you; among those that are born of women there is not a greater than John the Baptist; but he that is least in the kingdom of God is greater than he.

To what then shall I liken the men of this generation? And to what are they like?

They are like children sitting in the marketplace, and calling one to another, and saying we have piped to you and you have not danced, we have mourned to you and you have not wept.

For John the Baptist came neither eating bread neither drinking wine; and you say he has a devil.

The Son of man has come eating and drinking and you say; behold a gluttonous man and a winebibber, a friend of both publicans and sinners! But wisdom is justified of her children.

****

The Parable of the Creditors and Debtors

I have somewhat to say to you; There was a certain creditor which had two debtors; the one owed five hundred pence and the other fifty.

And when they had nothing to pay he frankly forgave them both. Tell me therefore which one will love him the most?

They said to him; the one who was forgiven the most. Jesus said, you have judged rightly.

Then he turned to the women who wiped his feet with her tears and anointed them with ointment. See this woman?

I entered into your house, and you gave me no water for my feet; but she has washed my feet with her tears and has wiped them with the hairs of her head.

You gave me no kiss but this woman has not ceased to kiss my feet since I came in.

My head with oil you did not anoint; but this woman has anointed my feet with ointment. Wherefore I say to you; her sins which be many are forgiven.

For she loved much, but to whom little is forgiven, the same loves little.

He said to her, your sins are forgiven; your faith has saved you, go in peace.

****

The Parable of the Sower

A sower went out to sow his seed; and as he sowed, some fell by the wayside; and it was trodden down and the fowls of the air devoured it.

And some did fall on a rock; and as soon as it had sprung up it withered away, because it lacked moisture.

And some fell among thorns; and the thorns grew along with it and choked it.

And other fell on good ground; and sprung up, and brought forth fruit a hundredfold. He that has ears to hear; let him hear.

Unto you it is given to know the mysteries of the kingdom of God.; but to others in parables; that seeing they might not see; and hearing they might not understand.

Now the parable is this; The seed is the word of God. Those by the wayside are they that hear.

Then comes the devil and takes away the word out of their hearts, lest they should believe and be saved.

They on the rock are they, which when they hear; receive the word with joy; and these have no root; which for awhile believe and in a time of temptation fall away.

And that which fell among thorns are they, which, when they have heard, go forth, and are choked with cares and riches and pleasures of this life, and bring no fruit to perfection.

But that which fell on good ground are they, which in an honest and good heart, having heard the word, keep it, and bring forth fruit with patience.

No man when he has lit a candle covers it with a vessel or hides it under a bed; but sets it on a candlestick that they which enter in may see the light.

For nothing is secret that shall not be made manifest; neither anything hid that shall not be known and come abroad.

Take heed therefore how you hear; for whoever has; to him shall be given; and from him that has not; shall be taken, even that which he seems to have.

My mother and my brethren are these which hear the word of God and do it.

****

Christ Commissions the Twelve

Take nothing for your journey, neither staves, nor scrip, neither bread, neither money; neither bring two coats each.

And whatever house you enter into; there abide and from there depart.

And whoever will not receive you, when you go out of that city, shake off the very dust from your feet for a testimony against them.

****

The Opinions of Who is Christ

He asked; Who do the people say that I am?

They said; some say John the Baptist, some say Elijah, and some say one of the old prophets has risen from the dead.

But who do you say I am? Peter said, You are the Christ of God.

****

Who is a Disciple?

The Son of man must suffer many things, and be rejected by the elders, and chief priests, and scribes, and be slain and be raised the third day.

If any man will come after me, let him deny himself, take up his cross daily, and follow me.

For whoever will save his life shall loose it; and whoever will loose his life for my sake shall save it.

For what advantage has a man if he gains the whole world and loses himself, or is cast away?

For whoever shall be ashamed of me and of my words, of him shall the Son of man be ashamed, when he shall come in his own glory, and in his Fathers, and of the holy angels.

But I tell you a truth, there are some standing here which shall not taste of death, until they see the kingdom of God.

****

The Disciples Powerlessness

The disciples are brought a mans son possessed of a devil and could do nothing with him.

Jesus than says; Oh faithless and perverse generation, how long shall I be with you, and suffer you?

Bring your son here. And immediately he cast the devil out of him.

Let these sayings sink down into your ears; for the Son of man shall be delivered into the hands of men.

****

The Ambitions of the Disciples

Whoever shall receive this little child in my name receives me; and whoever receives me receives him that sent me; for he that is least among you all, the same shall be great.

They asked him about a man they saw casting out devils in his name. And Jesus said to them; Forbid him not; for he that is not against us is for us.

You do not know what manner of spirit you are of. For the Son of man has not come to destroy men's lives, but to save them.

Foxes have holes, and the birds of the air have nests; but the Son of man has no place to lay his head. Then he said to another man; Follow me!

And he said to Jesus; Let me first go and bury my dead. Jesus said; Let the dead bury the dead; but you go and preach the kingdom of God.

No man having put his hand to the plow, and looking back is fit for the kingdom of God.

My Prayer….. May we daily Lord have the courage to speak of you, to those you bring into our lives… Amen

****

The Commission of the Seventy Others

The harvest is truly great, but the laborers are few; pray therefore to the Lord of the harvest that he would send forth laborers into his harvest.

Go your way; behold I send you forth as lambs among wolves. Carry neither a purse, nor scrip, nor shoes; and salute no man in the way.

And whatever house you enter, first say, peace be unto you. And if the Son of peace be there, your peace shall rest upon it; if not it shall return to you again.

And in the same house remain, eating and drinking such things as they give; for the laborer is worthy of his hire. Go not from house to house.

And in whatever city you enter and they receive you, eat such things as are set before you. And heal the sick which are there.

And say to them, The Kingdom of God has come near to you.

But in whatever city you enter, and they receive you not, go your ways out into the streets of the same city and say;

Even the very dust of your city which cleaves to us, we do wipe off against you; not withstanding be sure of this that the Kingdom of God has come near to you.

But I say to you that it shall be more tolerable in that day for Sodom and Gommorah, than for that city.

Woe unto you Choraizin! Woe unto you Bethsaida!

For if the mighty works had been done in Tyre and Sidon, which have been done in you, they would have a great while ago repented, sitting in sackcloth and ashes.

But it shall be more tolerable for Tyre and Sidon, than for you.

And you, Capernaum, which are exalted to heaven, shall be thrust down into hell. He that hears you hears me, and he that despises you, despises me and him that sent me.

****

The Return of the Seventy

I beheld Satan as it were, falling like lightning from heaven. Behold I give unto you power to tread on serpents and scorpions, and over all the power of the enemy; and nothing shall by any means hurt you.

Not withstanding in this rejoice not; that the spirits are subject to you, but rather that your names are written in heaven.

I thank you Father, Lord of heaven and earth, that you have hid these things from the wise and the prudent, and have revealed them to babes; even so Father, for so it seemed good in your sight.

All things are delivered to me by my Father; and no man knows who the Son is but the Father; and who the Father is but the Son, and he to whom the Son will reveal him.

Blessed are the eyes which see the things which you see.

For I tell you that many prophets and kings have desired to see the things which you see, and have not seen them; and to hear the things which you hear; and have not heard them.

****

The Lawyers Question

A certain Jewish lawyer came and said to Jesus; Master what shall I do to inherit eternal life? Jesus replied; What does it say in the law? Tell me what you have read.

The lawyer said; You shall love the Lord thy God with all your heart, and with all your soul, and with all your strength, and with all your mind, and your neighbor as yourself.

Jesus said to him; You have answered right; this do and you shall live. But he then said to Jesus; Who is my neighbor?

****

The Good Samaritan Parable

Jesus said to the lawyer this; A certain man went down from Jerusalem to Jericho and fell among thieves which stripped him of his clothing, and wounded him and departed, leaving him half dead.

And by chance there came down a certain priest that way; and when he saw him he passed by on the other side.

And likewise a Levite, when he came by that way, and saw him, he passed by on the other side as well.

But, a certain Samaritan, as he journeyed, came where he was and seeing him had compassion on him.

And went to him and bound up his wounds, pouring in oil and wine, and set him on his own beast, and brought him to an inn and took care of him.

And in the morning when he departed, he took out two pence and gave them to the host, and said to him, take care of him; and whatever you spend more, when I return this way I will repay you.

Which one of these three do you think was a neighbor to him who fell among thieves? And he said; He that showed mercy upon him. Jesus said, Go and do likewise yourself.

****

Martha's Home

Martha asks Christ why he doesn't care about her sister not helping her serve them. Jesus says to her; Martha, Martha, you are careful and troubled about many things.

But one thing is necessary; and your sister Mary has chosen that good thing, which shall not be taken away from her, for Mary had chosen to spend her time with the Lord.

****

The Lord's Prayer

When you pray say, Our Father, which art in heaven, Hallowed be thy name. Thy kingdom come thy will be done, as in heaven, so in earth. Give us day by day our daily bread.

And forgive us our sins; for we also forgive everyone that is indebted to us. And lead us not into temptation. But deliver us from evil.

Which of you shall have a friend, and shall go to him at midnight, and say to him, friend lend me three loaves; for a friend of mine in his journey has come to me, and I have nothing to set before him.

And he from within shall answer you and say; Trouble me not, the door is now shut, and my children are with me in bed; I cannot rise up and give it to you.

I say to you, though he can not rise and give it to him, because he is his friend, yet because of his importunity, he will rise and give him as many loaves as he needs.

And I say to you, ask and it shall be given to you; seek and you shall find; knock and it shall be opened to you.

For everyone that asks, receives; and he that seeks finds; and to him that knocks it shall be opened.

If a son asks bread of anyone of you that is a father, will he give him a stone? Or if he asks for a fish will he give him in place of the fish a serpent?

Or if he shall ask for an egg will he give him a scorpion?

If you then being evil, know how to give good gifts to your children; how much more shall your heavenly Father give the Holy Spirit to them that ask him?

****

The Dumb Demoniac is Healed

Every kingdom divided against itself is brought to desolation; and a house divided against itself shall fall. If Satan also be divided against himself how shall his kingdom stand?

Because you say that I cast out devils by Beelzebub. And if I by Beelzebub cast out devils, by whom do your sons cast them out? Therefore they shall be your judges.

But if I with the finger of God cast out devils, no doubt the kingdom of God has come upon you.

When a strong man armed keeps his palace, his goods are safe.

But when one stronger than he comes upon him, and overcomes him, he takes from him all his armor in which he trusted, and divides all his spoils.

He that is not with me is against me; and he that gathers not with me scatters abroad.

When an unclean spirit is cast out of a man, he walks through dry places seeking rest; and finding none he says, I will return to the house from which I came out.

And when he comes he finds it swept and garnished.

Then he goes and takes with him seven other spirits more wicked than himself; and they enter in and dwell there; and the last state of that man is worse than the first.

Blessed are they that hear the word of God and do it. This is an evil generation; they seek after a sign and there shall no sign be given, but the sign of Jonah the prophet.

For as Jonah was a sign to the Ninevites, so shall also the Son of man be to this generation.

The queen of the south shall rise up in judgment with the men of this generation, and condemn them; for she came from the uttermost parts of the earth to hear the wisdom of Solomon; and behold a greater than Solomon is here.

The men of Nineveh shall rise up in the judgment with this generation, and shall condemn it, for they repented at the preaching of Jonah, and behold a greater than Jonah is here.

No man when he has lighted a candle puts it in a secret place, neither under a bushel, but on a candlestick, that they which come in may see the light.

The light of the body is the eye; therefore also when your eye is single your whole body is full of light. but when your eye is evil your whole body is full of darkness.

Take heed therefore that the light which is in you be not darkness.

If your whole body therefore be full of light, having no part dark, the whole shall stand full of light, as when the bright shining of a candle gives you light.

****

Pharisaic Ceremonialism

Now you Pharisees do make clean the outside of the cup and the platter; but your inward part is full of ravening and wickedness.

You fools! Did not he which made that which is outside, make that which is inside also? But rather give alms of such things as you have; and behold, all things are clean unto you.

But woe unto you Pharisees For you give tithes of mint and rue and all manner of herbs, and passover judgment and the love of God; these things you should have done and not left the others undone.

Woe unto you Pharisees! For you love the uppermost seats in the synagogues, and greetings in the marketplaces. Woe unto you, scribes and Pharisses, hypocrites!

For you are as graves which appear not, and the men that walk over them are not aware of them.

Woe unto you also you lawyers! For you lay on men burdens which are grievous to be borne, and you yourselves touch not the burdens with the smallest of your fingers.

Woe unto you! For you build the tombs of the prophets, and your fathers killed them.

Truly you bear witness that you allowed the deeds of your fathers; for they indeed killed them, and you built their tombs.

Therefore also said the wisdom of God; I will send them prophets and apostles, and some of them they shall slay and persecute.

That the blood of all the prophets which was shed from the foundation of the world may be required of this generation.

From the blood of Able to the blood of Zacharias, which perished between the altar and the temple; truly I say to you, it shall be required of this generation.

Woe unto you lawyers! For you have taken away the key of knowledge; you entered not in yourselves, and to them which were entering you hindered them.

****

Christ Warns of False Doctrine

Beware of the leaven of the Pharisees, which is hypocrisy. For there is nothing covered that shall not be revealed; neither hid that shall not be known.

Therefore, whatever you have spoken in darkness shall be heard in the light; and that which you have spoken in the ear in closets, shall be proclaimed on the housetops.

And I say to you my friends, be not afraid of them that kill the body, and after that have nothing more they can do.

But I will forewarn you who you shall fear; fear him who after he has killed has the power to cast into hell; yes I say unto you, fear him.

Are not five sparrows sold for two farthings, and not one of them is forgotten before God. But even the very hairs of your head are all numbered.

Fear not therefore; for you are of more value than many sparrows.

Also I say to you, whoever shall confess me before men, him shall the Son of man confess before the angels of God.

But he that denies me before men shall be denied before the angels of God.

And whoever shall speak word against the Son of man, it shall be forgiven him; but to him that blasphemes against the Holy Ghost, it shall not be forgiven him.

And when they bring you to the synagogues, and to the magistrates, and powers, take no thought of what you shall say or how you will say it.

For the Holy Ghost shall teach you in that same hour what you should say.

****

The Parable of the Foolish Rich Man

A man from the company then asks Christ to speak to his brother about dividing his inheritance equally.

This is what he said; Man, who made me judge or divider over you?

Take heed and beware of covetousness. For a mans life consists not of the abundance of things which he posseses.

The ground of a certain rich man brought forth plentiful food.

And he thought within himself, what shall I do, because I do not have enough room to store all of my fruits?

And he said, this I will do; I will pull down my barns and build greater; and there I will store all of my fruits and my goods.

And I will say to my soul, soul, you have many goods laid up for many years, take it easy, eat, drink and be merry.

But God said to him; You fool! This night your soul shall be required of you; then whose shall those things be which you have provided?

So is he that stores up treasure for himself and is not rich towards God.

Therefore I say to you, take no thought for your life, what you shall eat, neither for the body, what you shall put on it.

The life is more than meat and the body is more than clothing.

Consider the ravens; for they neither sow seeds nor do they reap a harvest; neither do they have a storehouse or a barn; yet God feeds them; how much better are you then the fowls?

And which of you by taking thought can add so much as one cubit to his height?

If you then are not able to do that which is least, why take any thought for the rest?

Consider the lilies how they grow; they do not work neither do they toil; and yet I say to you; that Solomon in all his glory was not arrayed as one of these.

If God so clothes the grass, which today is in the field and tomorrow is cast into the oven; how much more will he clothe you, oh you of little faith?

And seek not what you shall eat, and what you shall drink, neither be of a doubtful mind.

For all these things do the nations of the world seek after; and your Father knows that you have need of these things.

But rather seek the kingdom of God and all these things will be added unto you.

Fear not, little flock; for it is your Fathers good pleasure to give you the kingdom.

Sell all that you have, and give alms; provide yourselves with bags that grow not old, a treasure in the heavens that doesn't fail, where no thief approaches neither does a moth corrupt it.

For where your treasure is, there will your heart be also. Let your loins be girded about, and your lights burning.

And you yourselves are like men who wait for their lord to return from a wedding; that when he comes, and knocks, they may open to him immediately.

Blessed are those servants who the Lord when he comes shall find watching; truly I say to you; that he shall gird himself, and have them sit down to dinner, and serve them himself.

And if he shall come in the second watch, or in the third watch, and find them so, blessed are those servants.

And this know; that if the goodman of the house had known what hour the thief would come, he would have watched and not allowed his house to be broken into.

Be you therefore ready also; for the Son of man comes in an hour when you think not.

Who then is a faithful and a wise steward, who his lord shall make the ruler over his household, to give them their portion of meat in due season?

Blessed is that's servant whom his lord shall find so doing at his coming. Truly I say to you; that he will make him ruler over all that he has.

But if that servant says in his heart; my lord delays his coming; and shall begin to beat the menservants and the maidens, and to eat and drink and be drunken.

The lord of that servant will come in a day when he is not looking for him, and at an hour when he is not aware, and will cut him in two; and appoint him his portion with the unbelievers.

And that servant who knew his lords will; and prepared not himself, neither did according to his will, shall be beaten with many stripes.

But he that knew not, and did things worthy of stripes, shall be beaten with few stripes. For to whom much is given, of him shall much be required.

And to whom men have committed much; of him they will ask even more. I have come to set a fire on earth; and what will I do if it is already kindled?

But I have a baptism to be baptized with; and how I am straightened until it is accomplished! Do you suppose that I have come to bring peace on earth? I tell you no! But rather to bring division.

For from hereon there shall be five in one house divided, three against two and two against three.

The father shall be divided against the son, and the son against the father; her mother against the daughter and the daughter against the mother; the mother in law against her daughter-in-law and the daughter in law against the mother in-law.

****

Lack of Discernment

When you see a cloud rising in the west you say a shower is coming, and so it is. And when you see the south wind blow you say; there will be heat and it comes to pass.

You hypocrites! You can discern the face of the sky and of the earth; but how is it that you do not discern this time? And why even among yourselves do you not judge that which is right?

When you go with your adversary to the magistrate, as you are in the way, give diligence that you may be delivered from him; unless he deliver you to the judge, and the judge to the officer, and the officer casts you into prison.

I tell you that you shall not depart from there until you pay the very last that you owe.

My Prayer...... May I at your coming be found doing your will in my life... Amen

****

Do Not Judge Harshly

Some Galileans had allowed their blood to be mixed with Pilates sacrifices.

Jesus begins by saying; Do you suppose that these Galileans were sinners above all Galileans because they allowed such things to happen?

I say to you no! And unless you repent, you shall in like manner perish.

Or those eighteen people upon whom the tower of Siloam fell, and killed them, do you suppose that they were sinners above all men that lived in Jerusalem?

I tell you no. But unless you repent, you shall in like manner perish.

A certain man had a fig tree planted in his vineyard; and he came and looked for fruit on it and found none.

The he said to the keeper of the vineyard; Behold these three years I came seeking fruit of this fig tree and found none; cut it down, why should it encumber the ground anymore?

And he answering said to the owner; Lord, leave it alone this year also, until I dig about it, and fertilize it; and if it bears fruit, good, but if not then you shall cut it down.

****

Jesus Heals a Woman on the Sabbath

He said to her; Woman you are loosed of your infirmity. The synagogue ruler complained of him healing her on the seventh day of the week, that being the Sabbath.

Jesus said; You hypocrite! Does not each one of you on the Sabbath let loose his ox or ass from the stall, and lead him away for watering?

And should not this woman being a daughter of Abraham whom Satan has bound for eighteen years, be set free from this bond on the Sabbath day?

****

The Parable of the Mustard Seed

What is the kingdom of God like? And to what shall I compare it to?

It is like a grain of mustard seed, which a man took, and cast it into his garden; and it grew and waxed into a great tree; and the birds of the air lodged in its branches.

To what else can I compare the kingdom of God to? It is like leaven, which a woman took and mixed into three measures of meal, until the whole mixture was leavened.

Strive to enter into the strait gate; for many I say to you shall try to enter in and will not be able to.

When at once the master of the house has risen up, and shut the door, and you begin to stand outside, and to knock at the door, saying, Lord, Lord, open up to us; and he shall answer you saying; I know not from where you are.

Then you shall begin to say. We have eaten and drunk in you presence, and you have taught in our streets.

But he shall say, I tell you, I know not from where you are; depart from me you workers of iniquity.

There shall be weeping and gnashing of teeth, when you shall see, Abraham, and Isaac, and Jacob, and all the prophets, in the kingdom of God, and you yourselves thrust out of it.

And they shall come from the east, and from the west, and from the north and from the south, and shall sit down in the kingdom of God.

And behold there are last which shall be first, and there are first which shall be last.

Some Pharisees come and tell Christ that he'd better leave because Herod will kill him.

Jesus said to them; you go and tell that fox, behold I cast out devils, and I do cures today and tomorrow, and the third day I shall be perfected.

Nevertheless I must walk today and tomorrow and the day following; for it cannot be that the prophet should perish outside of Jerusalem.

Oh Jerusalem, Jerusalem which kills the prophets, and stones them which are sent to you.

How often I have desired to gather thy children together, as a hen does gather her brood under her wings, but you would not have it.

Behold your house is left to you desolate; and truly I say to you, you shall not see me until the time come when you shall say, blessed is he that comes in the name of the Lord.

****

Jesus Heals a Man of the Dropsy

Is it lawful to heal on the Sabbath day? Which of you shall have an ass or an ox fall into a pit, and will not immediately pull him out on the Sabbath day? And he then healed the man.

****

He Rebukes the Prideful

When you are called of any man to a wedding, sit not down in the highest of rooms unless a more honorable man than you be called.

And after he has greeted him and you he comes to you and says; give this man your place and you begin with shame to take the lower room.

But when you are called, go and sit in the lower room, that when he who invited you comes he may say to you; Friend go up higher, then you shall have worship of them that eat with you.

For whoever exalts himself shall be abased; and he that humbles himself shall be exalted.

When you prepare a dinner or a supper, call not your friends or your brethren, neither your kinsmen nor your rich neighbors; lest they also invite you again and a recompense be made to you.

But when you prepare a feast call the poor, the maimed, the lame, and the blind.

And you shall be blessed; for they cannot repay you; and you shall be repayed at the resurrection of the just.

****

The Great Supper Parable

A certain man made a great supper, and invited many. And sent his servant at the time supper was ready to say to them who were invited; Come; for all things are now ready.

And they all with one consent began to make excuses. The first said to him; I have bought a piece of ground; and I must go and see it, please have me excused.

And another said I have bought five yolk of oxen; and I must go to prove them; please have me excused. And yet another said; I have married a wife and therefore I cannot come.

So that servant came and told his Lord those things. Than the master of the house being angry said to his servant; behold go quickly into the streets and lanes of the city, and bring in here the poor the needy the crippled and the blind.

And the servant said it has been done as you have commanded and yet there is still room.

And the lord then said to his servant; go out into the highways and the hedges, and compel them to come in that my house may be full.

For I say unto you, that none of those men which were first called shall taste of my supper.

If any man comes to me and hates not his father, and mother, and wife, and children, and brethren, and sisters and yes his own life also, he cannot be my disciple.

And whoever does not bear his cross and follow me, he cannot be my disciple.

For which one of you who intends to build a tower, does not sit down first, and count the cost, to determine if he has sufficient funds to finish it?

Unless haply, after he has laid the foundation, and is not able to finish it, all that have been watching him begin to mock him.

Saying this man began to build and was not able to finish it.

Or what king going to make war with another king, sits not down first, and consults whether he will be able with ten thousand to go up against he that comes at him with twenty thousand?

Or else while the other is still great way off he sends an ambassador to express a desire for peace.

So likewise, whoever there be among you that forsakes not all, cannot be my disciple.

Salt is good; but if the salt has lost its savour, with what can it be used to season?

It is fit for neither the land nor the compost heap; but all men cast it out. He that has ears to hear; let him hear.

My Prayer...... May my ears and eyes be spiritually open to your calling... Amen

****

The Parable of the Lost Sheep

What man among you, having one hundred sheep, if he lose one of them, does not leave the ninety nine in the wilderness, and go after the one which was lost, until he finds it?

And when he has found it, he lays it on his shoulders rejoicing. And when he comes home he calls together his friends and his neighbors, saying to them, rejoice with me; for I have found my sheep which was lost.

I say to you that likewise joy shall be in heaven over one sinner that repents, more than over ninety nine just persons which need no repentance.

Again what woman having ten pieces of silver, if she loses one piece, does not light a candle and sweep the house, and seek diligently until she finds it?

And when she has found it, she calls her friends and her neighbor's together saying, rejoice with me; for I have found the piece which I had lost.

Likewise I say to you, that there is joy in the presence of the angels over one sinner that repents.

****

The Prodigal Son

A certain man had two sons. And the younger of them said to his father; Father give to me the portion of goods that will be my inheritance. And he divided to them his living.

And not many days after that, the younger one gathered all his things together, and took his journey into a far country, and there wasted his substance with riotous living.

And when he had spent all, there arose a mighty famine in the land; and he began to be wanting.

And he went and joined himself to a citizen if that country; and he sent him into his fields to feed the swine.

And he longed that he himself could fill his own belly with the husks that the swine ate, but no man gave them to him.

And when he came to himself he said, How many hired servants of my father have bread enough and to spare, and I perish with hunger!

I will arise and go to my father, and say to him, father I have sinned against heaven and before you.

And I am no more worthy to be called your son; make me as one of your hired servants.

And he arose and came to his father. But when he was yet a great way off, his father saw him, and had compassion, and ran and fell on his neck and kissed him.

And the son said to him, father, I have sinned against heaven, and in your sight, and am no more worthy to be called your son.

But the father said to his servants, bring forth the best robe, and put it on him; and put a ring on his hand and shoes on his feet.

And bring here the fatted calf, and kill it; and let us eat and be merry. Now his elder son was in the field; and as he came and drew near to the house, he heard music and dancing.

And he called to one of the servants and asked what this commotion meant.

And he said to him, your brother has come back; and your father has killed the fatted calf, because he has received him safe and sound.

And he was angry and would not go in. Therefore his father came out and entreated him to come in.

And he answering said to his father, Lo these many years I have served you; neither did I transgress at any time your commandments.

And yet you never gave me a kid that I might make merry with my friends.

But as soon as this your son had come back, which had devoured your living with harlots; you have killed for him the fatted calf.

And he said to him; Son, you are always with me, and all that I have is yours.

It was right that we should make merry and be glad; for this man your brother was dead, and is alive again; and was lost, and now he is found.

****

The Parable of the Unjust Steward

There was a certain rich man who had an unjust steward; and the same was accused by him that he had wasted his goods.

And he called him and said to him; how is this that I hear of you? Give an account of your stewardship for you may no longer be steward.

Than the steward said within himself, what shall I do? For my lord will take away from me my stewardship; I cannot dig and to beg I am ashamed.

I am resolved as what to do, that when I am put out of my stewardship they will invite me into their houses.

So he called every one of his lords debtors to himself, and said to the first, how much do you owe to my lord?

And he said to him, one hundred measures of oil. And he said to him sit down quickly and write out fifty.

Then he said to another, How much do you owe? And he said to him one hundred measures of wheat. And he said to him, take your bill and write down fourscore.

And the lord commended the unjust steward for he had acted wisely; for the children of this world are wiser than the children of light.

And I say to you, make yourself friends of the mammon of unrighteousness; that when you fail; they may receive you into everlasting habitations.

He that is faithful in that which is least; is faithful in much; and he that is unjust in the least is unjust in the most also.

If you then have not been faithful in the unrighteous mammon, who will commit to your trust the true riches?

And if you have not been faithful in that which is another mans, who shall give you that which is you're own?

No servant can serve two masters; for he will either hate the one and love the other; or else he will hold to the one and despise the other. You cannot serve God and money.

****

The Covetous Pharisees are Derided

You are those who justify themselves before men; but God knows your hearts; for that which is highly esteemed among men is an abomination in the sight of God.

The law and the prophets were until John; Since that time the kingdom of God is preached and every man presses into it.

And it is easier for heaven and earth to pass than for one jot or title of the law to fail.

Whoever puts away his wife and marries another commits adultery; and whoever marries her that is put away from her husband commits adultery.

There was a certain rich man who was clothed in purple and fine linens, and faired sumptuously every day.

And there was a certain beggar named Lazarus, which was laid by his gate full of sores.

And he desired to be fed with the crumbs that fell from the rich man's table; moreover the dogs came and licked his sores.

And it came to pass that the beggar died, and was carried away by the angels to Abraham's bossum; the rich man also died and was buried.

And in hell he lifted up his eyes being tormented, and saw Abraham far off and Lazarus in his bosom.

And he cried and said, Father Abraham, have mercy on me, and send Lazarus that he may dip the tip of his finger, in the water and cool my tongue; for I am tormented in this flame.

But Abraham said; Son, remember that in your lifetime you did receive the good things, and Lazarus the evil things; but now he is comforted and you are tormented.

And besides all this, between us and you there is a great gulf fixed; so that they that would pass from here to you cannot;

neither can they pass to us that would come from there to here.

And he said to him; I pray thee therefore father that you would send him to my father's house; for I have five brethren that he may testify to them; unless they also may come to this place of torment.

Abraham said to him; they have Moses and the prophets; let them hear them.

And he said to him no Father Abraham; but if one went to them from the dead they would repent.

And he said to him, if they will not hear Moses and the prophets, neither will they be persuaded, though one rose from the dead.

****

His Warnings Against Stumbling Blocks

It is impossible to think that offences will not come; but woe unto him by whom they come!

It were better for him that a millstone were hung around his neck, and he were cast into the sea, than he should offend one of these little ones.

Take heed to yourselves. If your brother trespasses against you, rebuke him; and if he repents forgive him.

And if he trespasses against you seven times in a day, and seven times in a day turns to you again, saying, I repent; you shall forgive him.

If you had faith as a grain of mustard seed, you might say to this sycamore tree; Be plucked up by the roots and be planted in the sea; and it would obey you.

But which of you having a servant plowing or feeding cattle, will say to him by and by, when he has come from the field; go ands sit down for dinner?

And will not rather say to him; make the food ready that I may eat.

And gird yourself and serve me, until I have eaten and drunk and afterward you may serve yourself.

Does he thank the servant because he has done the things commanded of him? I think not.

So likewise you, when you shall have done all those things which are commanded of you, say, we are unprofitable servants; we have done that which was our duty to do so.

Ten lepers were healed by Christ; Jesus said to them; go and show yourselves to the priests.

One of them who was a Samaritan returned to thank him and to worship, Jesus said; Were there not ten cleansed? But where are the other nine?

There are not found any that returned to give glory to God except this stranger.

Arise go your way; your faith has made your whole.

Then a Pharisee demanded to know when the kingdom of God would come; He said; The kingdom of God comes not by observation.

Neither shall they say; here it is or there it is; for the kingdom of God is within you.

****

His Second Coming is Foretold

The days will come when you shall desire to see one of the days of the Son of man and shall not be able to see it.

And they shall say to you; see here. or see there, do not follow them or go after them.

For as lightening that begins under one part of heaven and shines under another part of the heavens; so shall also the Son of man be in his day.

But first he must suffer many things and be rejected of this generation. And as it was in the days of Noah; so shall it also be in the day of the Son of man.

They did eat, they drank, they married wives, they were given in marriage, until the day that Noah entered into the ark, and the flood came and destroyed them all.

Likewise also it was in the days of Lot; they did eat, they drank, they bought, they sold, they planted and they built.

But the same day that Lot went out of Sodom it rained fire and brimstone from heaven and destroyed them all.

Even thus shall it be in the day that the Son of man shall be revealed.

In that day; he which shall be upon the housetop, and his things in the house, let him not come down to take them away; and he that is in the field let him likewise not turn back.

Remember Lots wife? Whoever shall seek to save his life shall lose it, and whoever shall lose his life shall preserve it.

I tell you in that night; two men shall be in one bed; the one shall be taken and the other shall be left.

Two women shall be grinding together; the one shall be taken and the other left. Two men shall be in the field; the one shall be taken and the other left.

Then he said; wherever the body is, there will the eagles be gathered together.

****

The Parable of the Unjust Judge

There was in a certain city a judge which did not fear God. Neither did he have any regard for man. And there was a widow in that city, and she came to him and said; avenge me of my adversary.

And he would not for a while; but afterwards he said within himself; Though I fear not God nor do I regard man, yet because this widow troubles me I will avenge her, to keep her from continually coming to me and wearying me.

Hear what the unjust judge said. And shall not God avenge his own elect which cry to him night and day? Though he bears a long time with them?

I tell you that he will avenge them speedily, Never the less, when the Son of man comes, will he find faith on the earth?

****

The Parable of the Pharisee and the Publican

Two men went up to the temple to pray; the one was a Pharisee and the other was a publican.

The Pharisee stood up and prayed this way by himself, God, I thank thee that I am not as other men are, extortioners, unjust, adulterers, or even as this publican.

I fast twice a week and give tithes of all that I possess. And the publican standing far off would not so much as lift up his eyes toward heaven.

But he smote himself upon the breast, saying, God be merciful to me a sinner.

I tell you that this man went down to his house justified, rather than the other; for everyone that exalts himself shall be abased; and he that humbles himself shall be exalted.

****

Christ and the Children

Some people approached Jesus with little children and babes that he might touch them. The apostles when they saw this rebuked them.

Then Jesus said; Suffer little children to come to me and forbid them not for of such is the kingdom of God.

Truly I say to you, whoever can not receive the kingdom of God as a little child, shall in no way enter into it.

With that a certain rich young ruler asked Christ; Good Master; what shall I do to inherit eternal life? Jesus said to him; Why do you call me good?

There is none that is good except one and that is God. You know the commandments, Do not commit adultery, Do not kill, Do not steal, Do not bear false witness, Honor your father and your mother.

He then said to Jesus; all these things have I done from my youth.

Yet you lack one thing; Sell all that you have, and distribute it to the poor and you shall have treasure in heaven; come and follow me.

How hardly shall they that have riches enter into the kingdom of God! Nevertheless, the things which are impossible with men are possible with God.

Truly I say to you, there is no man that has left house or parents, or bretheren, or wife, or children, for the kingdom of God's sake; who shall not receive manifold more in this present time, and in the world to come life everlasting.

Behold we go up to Jerusalem, and all things that are written by the prophets concerning the Son of man shall be accomplished.

For he shall be delivered to the Gentiles, and be mocked and be spitefully treated, and spit upon. And they shall scourge him, and put him to death, and the third day he shall rise again.

****

A Blind Beggar Shouts to Christ

What do you want that I should do for you? And he said that I may receive my sight. And Jesus said; Receive your sight, your faith has made you whole.

****

The Calling of Zacchaeus

A man short in stature climbs into a tree to see Christ as he passes by. Jesus said to him; Zacchaeus, make haste, and come down, for today I must abide in your house.

As He comes down and meets Jesus face to face, Jesus says to him; this day has salvation come to you're household, inasmuch as you also are a son of Abraham.

For the Son of man has come to seek and to save that which was lost.

****

The Parable of the Pounds

A certain nobleman went into a far country to receive for himself a kingdom, and to return. And he called his ten servants and delivered unto them ten pounds and said to them, occupy until I return.

But his citizens hated him, and sent a message after him, saying, we will not have this man reign over us.

And it came to pass, that when he had returned, having received the kingdom, then he commanded to have these servants brought to him, to whom he had given the money, that he might know how much every man had gained through trading.

Then the first man came and said, lord thy pound has gained ten pounds. And he said to him, well done thy good servant; because you have been faithful in very little, I give you authority over ten cities.

And the second man came saying; lord thy pound has gained five pounds. He said likewise to him; be thou ruler over five cities.

And another one came and said lord, here is your pound which I have kept laid up in a napkin.

For I feared you because you are an austere man. You take up that which you have not layed down, and you reap that which you have not sown.

And he said to him, out of your own mouth will I judge you, you wicked servant.

You knew that I was an austere man, taking up that I laid not down, and reaping that which I have not sown.

Wherefore then, why did you not give the money to the bank, that at my coming I might have received my own with interest?

And he said to them which stood by; take from him the pound which he has and give it to him that has ten pounds.

And they said to him; but lord he already has ten pounds. For I say to you to everyone who has shall more be given; and from him that has not; even that which he has shall be taken away.

But those enemies, which desired that I would not reign over them, bring them here and slay them before me.

****

Christ's Entry into Jerusalem

Go you into the village over against you; in the which at your entering you will find a colt tied; whereupon never a man has sat; loose him and bring him here.

And if any man asks you why did you loose him? You shall say to him, because the Lord has need of him.

As Jesus rode into the city, some of the Pharisees said to him, Master rebuke your disciples, for all were praising him and worshiping him.

Jesus said to them; I tell you that if these should hold their peace, the stones would immediately cry out.

****

Jesus Weeps Over Jerusalem

If you had known, even you, at least in this your day, the things which belong to your peace! But now they are hid from your eyes.

For the days shall come upon you, that your enemies shall cast a trench about you, and encompass you round about, and keep you in on every side.

And they shall lay you even with the ground, and your children with you; and they shall not leave one stone upon another; because you knew not the time of your visitation.

And then Christ went into the temple and began to cast them out who were selling within God's house. He then said; It is written; My house is the house of prayer; but you have made it a den of thieves.

****

Christ's Authority is Challenged

And as Jesus was teaching in the temple one day; some of the chief priests, scribes and elders asked Christ by whose authority he was doing these things?

Jesus said; I will ask you one thing; and answer me; The baptism of John, was it from heaven or of men?

They would not answer Him; Jesus said; Neither will I tell you by what authority I do these things.

****

The Parable of the Wicked Husbandmen

A certain man planted a vineyard, and lent it out to husbandmen, and went into a far country for a long time.

And at the season he sent a servant to the husbandmen, that they should give him of the fruit of the vineyard; but the husbandmen beat him and sent him away empty.

And again he sent them another servant and they beat him also; and treated him shamefully, and sent him away empty also.

And again he sent a third; and they wounded him also, and cast him out. Then said the lord of that vineyard, what shall I do?

I will send my beloved son; it may be that they will reverence him when they see him.

But when the husbandmen saw him they reasoned among themselves, saying, this is the heir; come let us kill him, that the inheritance may be ours.

So they cast him out of the vineyard and killed him. What therefore shall the lord of that vineyard do to them?

He shall come and destroy these husbandmen and give the vineyard to others.

What is this then that is written; The stone which the builders rejected; the same has become the head of the corner?

Whoever shall fall upon that stone shall be broken; but on whoever it shall fall, shall be ground to powder.

****

The Question of Paying Tribute to Caesar

Why do you tempt me? Show me a penny. Who's image and superscription is on it? Render therefore unto Caesar the things which are Caesars, and to God, the things which are God's.

****

They Attempt to Trap Christ

The children of this world marry and are given in marriage.

But they which shall be accounted worthy to obtain that world, and the resurrection from the dead, neither marry nor are they given in marriage.

Neither can they die anymore; for they are equal to the angels; and are the children of God being the children of the resurrection.

Now that the dead are raised, even Moses showed at the bush, when he called the Lord, the God of Abraham, and the God of Isaac, and the God of Jacob.

For He is not a God of the dead, but of the living.

****

Jesus Poses a Question to the Jews

How do you say that Christ is David's son?

And David himself said in the book of Psalms;

The Lord said unto my Lord; sit thou on my right hand, until I make your enemies your footstool. David therefore calls him Lord, how then can he be his son?

Beware of the scribes, which love to walk in long robes, and love greetings in the markets, and the highest seats in the synagogues, and the chief rooms at feasts.

Which devour widow's houses, and for a show make long prayers; the same shall receive the greater damnation.

My Prayer….. Blessed be the name of the Lord God Almighty, Blessed be your name forever… Amen

****

The Widows Mite

After observing a widow putting into the treasury a small coin, the last of her money, Jesus said this; Of a truth I say to you, that this poor widow has put more in then them all.

For all of these have out of their abundance cast into the offerings of God; but she out of her penury has cast in all the living she had.

****

Foretelling of the Temples Destruction

As for these things which you behold, the days will come, in the which there shall not be left one stone standing upon another that shall not be thrown down.

Take heed that you be not deceived. For many shall come in my name saying; I am Christ; and the time draws near; go not therefore after them.

But when you shall hear of wars and commotions, be not terrified for these things must first come to pass; but the end is not by and by.

Nation shall rise against nation, and kingdom against kingdom. And great earthquakes shall be in divers places, and famines and pestilences; and fearful signs, and great signs shall there be from heaven.

But before all these they shall lay their hands on you, and persecute you, delivering you up to synagogues, and into prisons, being brought before kings and rulers for my names sake.

And it shall turn to you for a testimony.

Settle it therefore in you hearts, not to meditate before what you shall answer. For I will give you a mouth and wisdom.

Which all of your adversaries shall not be able to gainsay nor resist. And you shall be betrayed by both parents, and bretheren, and kinsfolks, and friends; and some of you shall they cause to be put to death.

And you shall be hated of all men for my namesake.

But there shall not so much as a hair of your head perish. In your patience you possess your souls. And when you shall see Jerusalem encircled with armies, then know that the desolation thereof is near.

Then let them which are in Judae, flee into the mountains; and let them which are in the midst of it depart out of it, and let them not that are in the countries enter therein.

For these be the days of vengeance, that all things which are written will be fulfilled. But woe unto them that are with child, and to them that give suck in those days!

For there shall be great distress in the land, and wrath upon this people.

And they shall fall by the edge of the sword, and shall be led away captive to all nations; and Jerusalem shall be trodden down by the Gentiles until the time of the Gentiles be fulfilled.

And there shall be signs in the sun, and in the moon, and in the stars; and upon the earth distress of nations with perplexity; the sea and the waves roaring, mens hearts failing them for fear, and looking after those things which are coming on the earth; for the powers of heaven shall be shaken.

And then shall they see the Son of man coming in a cloud with power and with great glory.

And when these things begin to come to pass, then look up, and lift up your heads; for your redemption draws near.

Behold the fig tree, and all the trees. When they shoot forth you both see and know of yourselves that summer is near.

So likewise when you see these things come to pass, know that the kingdom of God is near at hand.

Truly I say to you, that this generation shall not pass until all things are fulfilled. Heaven and earth shall pass away; but my words will never pass away.

And take heed of yourselves unless at anytime your hearts be overcharged with surfeiting, and drunkenness, and the cares of this life that this day come upon you unaware.

For as a snare shall it come upon them that dwell upon the face of the whole earth.

Watch therefore, and pray always, that you may be accounted worthy to escape all of these things, that shall come to pass; and shall be found worthy to stand before the Son of man.

****

Preparing the Passover

Go and prepare us the Passover that we may eat. Behold, when you have entered into the city, there shall a man meet you bearing a pitcher of water; follow him into the house he enters into.

And you shall say to the Goodman of the house; the Master says unto you, where is the guest chamber? Where I shall eat the Passover with my disciples?

And he shall show you a large furnished upper room; there you will make ready for the feast.

With desire I have desired to eat this Passover with you before I suffer; For I say to you; I will not eat this anymore until it is fulfilled in the kingdom of God.

Take this and divide it among yourselves. For I say to you, I will not drink of the fruit of the vine, until the kingdom of God shall come.

This is my body; which is given for you, do this in memory of me.

This is the cup of the new testament in my blood, which is shed for you. But behold; the hand of him who betrays me is with me on the table.

And truly the Son of man will go, as it was determined; but woe to that man by whom he is betrayed!

****

God's Kingdom

The kings of the Gentiles exercise lordship over them; and they that exercise lordship over them are called benefactors.

But you shall not be so. But he that is greatest among you, let him be as the younger; and he that is chief as he that serves.

You are they which have continued with me in my temptations. And I appoint to you a kingdom; as my Father has appointed me.

That you may eat and drink with me at my table in my kingdom, and sit on thrones judging the twelve tribes of Israel.

Simon, Simon, behold, Satan has desired to have you, that he may sift you as wheat; but I have prayed for you, that your faith fails not; and when you are converted, strengthen your brethren.

I tell you Peter; the cock shall not crow this day; before you have denied three times that you know me.

When I sent you without purse, and scrip, and shoes, did you lack anything?

But now, he that has a purse, take it, and likewise his scrip; and he that has no sword, let him sell his garment and buy one.

For I say to you, that this that is written must yet be accomplished in me. And he was reckoned among the transgressors; for the things concerning me have an end. It is enough.

****

The Garden of Gethsemane

Pray that you enter not into temptation. Father, if you are willing, remove this cup from me; nevertheless not my will but thine be done.

Why do you sleep? Rise up and pray, unless you enter into temptation.

While Jesus was speaking, Judas came with the soldiers and others with him. And he walked up and kissed Christ. Jesus said; Judas, do you betray the Son of, man with a kiss?

Have you come out against me as you would a thief, with swords and staves?

When I was daily with you in the temple, you stretched forth no hands against me; but this is your hour and the power of darkness.

****

Christ Before the Chief Counsel

When brought before Pilate Jesus was asked how he would answer the accusations that were made against him. And he said; If I tell you, you will not believe. And if I ask you, you will not answer me, nor will you let me go. Hereafter, the Son of man shall sit on the right hand of the power of God.

They then said to Him; Are you the Son of God; He said; You say that I am.

****

Christ Addresses the Women

Daughters of Jerusalem; weep not for me, but weep for yourselves, and for your children.

For behold the days are coming, in the which they shall say, blessed are the barren, and the wombs which never bare, and the pap's which never gave suck.

Then shall they begin to say to the mountains, fall on us, and to the hills, cover us.

For if they do these things in a green tree, what shall be done in the dry?

On the cross, Jesus said; Father forgive them, for they know not what they are doing.

Later on he said to the thief next to him; Truly I say unto you; this day you shall be with me in paradise.

And with His dying breath he said; Father into your hands I commend my spirit.

My Prayer….. Lord, help me this day to pick up my cross and follow you. Protect us this day, and deliver us from evil… Amen

****

Christ Meets the Disciples

Two of the disciples were on the road to Emmaus after Christ's death; and as they were talking Jesus came along side of them and walked along with them; their eyes were unable to recognize him.

What manner of communications are these that you have with each other, as you walk, and are sad?

They said to him, have you not heard of what happened in Jerusalem? Jesus said; What thing?

And they expounded to him about his own death and crucifixion, and how the tomb was found empty with an angel sitting by it.

Then Jesus said to them; O fools and slow of heart to believe all that which the prophets have spoken.

Ought not Christ to have suffered these things, and to enter into his glory? Their eyes still being closed to who it was that spoke to them.

****

Christ Appears to the Eleven Apostles

Peace be unto you! With that they were extremely afraid, and Jesus said; Why are you troubled?

And why do thoughts arise in your hearts? Behold my hands and my feet, that it is I myself; handle me and see; for a spirit has not flesh and bones as you see me have.

Jesus then said to them; Have you any meat?

These are the words, which I spoke to you while I was yet with you, that all things must be fulfilled, which were written in the law of Moses, and in the prophets, and in the psalms, concerning me.

Then he opened their understanding and said to them; Thus it is written, and thus it behooved Christ to suffer, and to rise from the dead the third day.

And that repentance and remittance of sins; should be preached in his name among all nations, beginning at Jerusalem. And you are witnesses of these things.

And behold I send the promise of my Father upon you; but wait here in the city of Jerusalem, until you are endowed with power from on high.

From the Gospel of Saint John

John's Disciples Seek Out Christ

Two of John the Baptists disciples come to follow Christ. He says to them; What is it you seek? They then said; Where do you live? And Jesus said; Come and see.

And there they stayed with him for the day. Then Andrew left and brought back his brother, Simon Peter.

Christ seeing him said; You are Simon the son of Jona; you shall be called Cephas, which being interpreted means a stone.

The following day Christ found Philip, and said to him; follow me.

Then Philip said to Nathaniel that they had found the messiah of Galilee, and he said, can anything good come out of Galilee? Nathaniel said to him; come and see.

Jesus seeing Nathaniel said; Behold an Israelite indeed in whom there is no guile.

Nathaniel said, How is it you know me? And Christ said to him; Before Philip called you, when you were under the fig tree, I saw you.

Philip said; truly you are the Son of God, the King of Israel.

Jesus answered saying; Because I answered you saying that I saw you under a fig tree, you believe? You shall see greater things than these.

Truly I say to you, Hereafter you shall see heaven open, and the angels of God ascending and descending upon the Son of man.

****

The First Miracle

At the wedding of Cana, the people came to Mary, the mother of Jesus, to tell her that they had run out of wine and she told Jesus.

He said to her; Woman, what have I to do with you? My hour has not yet come. Then she said to the servants; Whatever he tells you to do, do it.

Christ said; Fill the water pots with water. Then He said; Now draw some out and give it to the governor of the feast. The governor said that the best wine had been saved for last. Not knowing where it had come from. This was Christ's first miracle.

****

Christ in the Temple

After Jesus had made a scourge of small cords, he drove all out of the temple and overthrew the tables of the moneychangers.

And he said to them; Take these things out from here, do not make my Fathers house a house of merchandise.

Then they questioned his authority, to which Jesus said; Destroy this temple, and in three days I will raise it up.

****

Christ the Teacher

Truly, truly I say to you, except a man be born again, he cannot see the kingdom of God. Truly I say unto you; except a man be born of water and of the Spirit, he cannot enter into the kingdom of God.

That which is born of the flesh is flesh, and that which is born of the Spirit, is spirit. Marvel not, that I say to you, that you must be born again.

The wind blows where it will, and you hear the sound of it, but you don't know from where it came, and where it is going; so is everyone who is born of the Spirit.

****

The Ignorance of Nicodemus

He said to Jesus; How can these things be? How can a man be born when he is old? Can he enter again into his mother's womb?

Jesus replied; Are you not a master of Israel, and you don't know these things?

Truly, truly, I say to you; that we speak those things which we do know, and testify that we have seen; and you receive not our witness.

If I have told you earthly things and you believe not; how shall you believe heavenly things?

And no man has ascended up to heaven, but he that came down from heaven, even the Son of man which is in heaven.

****

Salvations Conditions

And as Moses lifted up the serpent in the wilderness; even so must the Son of man be lifted up.

That whosoever believes in him should not perish but have eternal life.

For God so loved the world, that he gave his only begotten Son, that whoever believes in him should not perish, but have everlasting life.

For God did not send his son into the world to condemn the world; but that the world through him might be saved.

He that believes in him is not condemned; but he that believes not in him is condemned already, because he has not believed in the name of the only begotten Son of God.

And this is the condemnation, that light has come into he world, and men loved darkness rather than light, because their deeds were evil.

For everyone that does evil, hates the light, neither will he come to the light, lest his deeds should be reproved.

But he that does truth comes to the light that his deeds may be made manifest, that they are worked in God.

****

The Samaritan Woman

While Jesus was sitting by Jacobs well, there came a woman from Samaria, Jesus said to her; Give me to drink.

The woman replied; How is it that you being a Jew, asks me a Samarian woman, to give you a drink?

The Jews have no dealings with the Samaritans.

Jesus said; If you knew the gift of God, and who it is that said to you, give me a drink, you would have asked of him and he would have given you living water.

She said to him; you have nothing to draw up water with and the well is deep, from where will you get this living water?

Are you greater than our father Jacob, who gave us this well, and drank from it himself, and his children, and his cattle?

Jesus said to her; Whoever drinks of this water shall thirst again; But whoever drinks of the water that I shall give him, shall never thirst again; but the water that I shall give him shall be in him a well of water springing up into everlasting life.

The woman said to him, Sir give me this water that I thirst not, neither do I come here to draw anymore.

Jesus said to her; go and call your husband and come here. She said to him; I have no husband.

He said to her; You have well said that you have no husband. For you have had five husbands; and he whom you have now is not your husband. In that you have spoken truly.

The woman said to him, Sir, I perceive that you are a prophet. He said; woman, believe me, that the hour is coming when you shall neither in this mountain, nor at Jerusalem, worship the Father.

You worship something that you know not; we know what we worship, for salvation is of the Jews.

But the hour is coming, when the true worshippers shall worship the Father in spirit and in truth. For the Father seeks such to worship Him.

God is a Spirit and they that worship Him must worship Him in spirit and in truth.

She said, I know that Messiah is coming, which is called Christ, and when he has come he will tell us all things.

He said to her; I that speak to you am he.

With that she ran to tell all about her encounter with the Lord. In the mean time his disciples said to him, come and eat.

And he said; I have meat to eat that you know not of.

His disciples said; Has anyone brought Him any meat? Christ said; My meat is to do the will of him that sent me, and to finish his work.

Do you not say that there are yet four months until the harvest? Behold, I say unto you to lift up your eyes and look on the fields; for they are white and already to harvest.

And he that reaps receives wages, and gathers fruit unto life eternal; that both he that sows and he that reaps may rejoice together.

And in this is that saying true; one sows and another man reaps. I sent you to reap that which you put no labor into, other men labored and you have entered into their labors.

****

Christ Heals the Son of a Nobleman

A nobleman of Cana, hearing that Christ was there came to see him. And when he found him he said; Would you please come and heal my son, for he is at the point of death?

Jesus said to him; Unless you see signs and wonders you will not believe. He said, please come with me or my son will die. Christ said; Go your way, your son lives.

****

Healing at the Pool of Bethsaida

At the pool Christ sees a man who had been sick for thirty eight years. He said to him; Will you be made whole?

He said, Sir I have no man to put me in the water when it is stirring. For at this well at a certain hour of the day, whoever got into the water was healed.

But he said; When the water is troubled before I can get into it, another gets in before me. Jesus said to him; Rise, take up your bed and walk.

The Jews started to murmur that he had healed on the Sabbath day. The man did not know it was Jesus for he had scurried away.

Later Christ found the man and said to him; Behold you have been made whole; go and sin no more, unless a worse thing come upon you.

****

The Jews Seek to Slay Him

Jesus answered them in this way; My Father worked up until now, and I work. They were enraged, because not only did he heal of the Sabbath, but, he said that God was his father, making himself, equal with God.

Christ said; Truly, truly, I say to you, the Son can do nothing of himself, but, what he sees the Father doing; For whatever things the Father does these things the Son does also.

For the Father loves the Son, and shows him all the things that he himself does. And he will show him greater works than these that you may marvel.

For as the Father raises up the dead; and quickens them; even so the Son quickens whom he will. For the Father judges no man; but has committed all judgment to the Son.

That all men should honor the Son, even as they honor the Father. He that does not honor the Son honors not the Father who sent him.

Truly, truly I say to you, he that hears my words, and believes in him that sent me has everlasting life and shall not come into condemnation; but is passed from death into life.

Truly, truly, I say to you, the hour is coming, and now is, when the dead shall hear the voice of the Son of God; and they that hear shall live.

For as the Father has life in himself; so has he given to the Son to have life in himself. And he has given him authority to execute judgment also, because he is the Son of man.

Marvel not at this; for the hour is coming, in which all that are in the graves shall hear his voice.

And they shall come forth from the grave; they that have done good to the resurrection of eternal life; and they that have done evil to the resurrection of damnation.

I can of my own self do nothing; as I hear; I judge and my judgment is just; because I seek not my own will; but the will of my Father who sent me.

If I bear witness of myself, my witness is not true. There is another that bears witness of me; and I know that the witness that he bears of me is true.

You sent to John, and he bore witness to the truth. But I receive not testimony from man; but these things I say that you might be saved.

He was a burning and a shining light; and you were willing for a season to rejoice in his light.

But I have a greater witness than that of John; for the works which the Father has given me to finish, the same works that I do, bear witness of me, that the Father has sent me.

And the Father himself which has sent me, has bore witness of me. You have neither heard his voice at any time, nor have you seen his shape.

And you do not have his word abiding in you; for whom he has sent you believe not.

Search the scriptures, for in them you think that you have eternal life; and they are they which testify of me. And you will not come to me that you may have eternal life.

I receive not honor from men. But I know you, that you do not have the love of God in you.

I have come in my Fathers name and you receive me not; if another should come in his own name; him you would receive.

How can you believe which receive honor from one another, and seek not the honor which comes from God only?

Do not think that I will accuse you to the Father; there is on that accuses you; even Moses in whom you trust.

For had you believed Moses, you would have believed in me, for he wrote of me. But if you believe not his writings, how shall you believe my words?

My Prayer….. Oh Lord. This day may I stay true to your word. Ever faithful, believing that which you have said, you will accomplish in my life… Amen

****

Feeding Five Thousand

Jesus looked at the great crowd, and He said to his disciples; From where shall we buy bread that these may eat?

This he said already knowing what he would do.

Then one of the disciples, Andrew said; One small boy has five barley loaves and two small fish.

Jesus then said; Make the men sit down. Jesus then gave thanks and told his disciples to distribute food to everyone.

And when they were done they gathered together twelve baskets above and beyond what had been eaten. Later the disciples went down by the sea and took a boat to cross to the other side.

During the night Christ came to them walking on the water. Upon seeing him they were afraid and Jesus said to them; It is I, be not afraid.

****

At Capernaum

Later that day having reached the other side, the people had already arrived looking for Jesus in Capernaum.

After finding Him, they said, Rabbi, when did you come here? Jesus said; Truly, truly, I say to you; You seek me not because you saw the miracles, but because you did eat of the loaves and were filled.

Labor not for the meat which perishes, but for that meat which endures to everlasting life, which the Son of man shall give to you; for him has God the father sealed.

This is the work of God; that you believe in him, whom he has sent.

****

The Bread of Life

Truly, truly I say to you, Moses did not give you that bread from heaven; but my Father gives you that true bread from heaven.

For the bread of God is he which came down from heaven, and gives life to the world.

I am the bread of life; he that comes to me shall never hunger; and he that believes in me shall never thirst.

But I say to you; that you also have seen me and believe not.

All that the Father gives me shall come to me; and him that comes to me, I will in no way cast out. For I came down from heaven not to do my own will, but the will of him that sent me.

And this is the Fathers will which has sent me, that of all which he has given me, I should lose nothing, but should raise it up again on the last day.

And this is the will of Him that sent me that everyone which sees the Son, and believes in him, may have everlasting life; and I will raise him up on the last day.

****

The Jews Challenge Him

Murmur not among you. No man can come to me except the Father who has sent me draw him; and I will raise him up on the last day.

It is written in the prophets; and they shall be taught of God. Every man therefore that has heard, and has learned of the Father shall come to me.

Not that any man has seen the Father, except he which is of God, he has seen the Father. Truly I say to you, he that believes in me has everlasting life.

I am the bread of life. Your fathers did eat manna in the wilderness, and are dead.

This is the bread which came down from heaven; if any man eats of this bread he shall live forever; and the bread which I shall give is my flesh, which I will give for the life of the world.

Truly I say to you; Unless you eat the flesh of the Son of man, and drink his blood, you have no life in you.

Whoever eats my flesh and drinks my blood has eternal life; and I will raise him up on the last day. For my flesh is meat indeed and my blood is drink indeed.

He that eats my flesh and drinks my blood dwells in me and I in him. As the living Father has sent me; and I live by the Father, he that eats me, even he shall live by me.

This is that bread which came down from heaven; not as your fathers did eat manna, and are dead; he that eats of this bread shall live forever.

****

Truths are Misunderstood

Does this offend you? What and if you shall se the Son of man ascend up to where he was before?

It is the Spirit that quickens; the flesh profits for nothing; the words that I speak to you; they are spirit and they are life.

But there are some of you that believe not. Therefore I said to you, that no man can come to me, except it was given to him of my Father. Many started leaving him after this.

Than Jesus turned to the twelve and said; will you also go away? And they said no. Jesus said; Have I not chosen you; and one of you is a devil?

****

His Brethren Question Him

His brethren said to him; Depart from here and go to Judea that your disciples may also see the works that you do.

For there is no man that does things in secret, and he himself seeks not to be known openly. If you do these things go and show yourself to the world.

For neither did his brethren believe him. Jesus then said; My time has not yet come, but your time is always ready.

The world cannot hate you; but me it hates, because I testify of it, that the works thereof are evil. You go up to this feast; I will not go up to the feast, for my time has not yet fully come.

****

The Challenge to Unbelievers

My doctrine is not mine, but his that sent me. If any man will do his will, he shall know of the doctrine, whether it is of God, or if I speak of myself.

He that speaks of himself seeks his own glory; but he that seeks his glory that sent him; the same is true, and no unrighteousness is in him.

Did not Moses give you the law, and yet not one of you keeps the law? Why do you go about to kill me? Then they said to him; you have a devil, who is looking to kill you?

I have done one work and you all marvel. Moses therefore gave to you circumcision, not because it is of Moses but the Father; and you on the Sabbath day circumcise a man.

If a man on the Sabbath day receives circumcision, that the law of Moses should not be broken; are you angry at me because I have made a man every bit whole on the Sabbath?

Judge not according to the appearance, but judge a righteous judgment.

****

Christ Speaks of His Death

Yet a little while am I with you, and then I will go to him that sent me. You shall seek me and not find me; and where I am you cannot come.

If any man thirsts, let him come to me and drink. He that believes in me, as the scripture has said, out of his belly shall flow rivers of living water.

****

A Woman Caught in Adultery

They brought a woman before him caught in the act of adultery to tempt him saying; Moses in the law commanded us, that such a person should be stoned; What do you say?

Jesus stood up and said to them; He that is without sin among you let him first throw a stone at her.

They walked away leaving Christ alone with the woman; He said to her; Woman, where are your accusers? Has no man condemned you?

She said no man Lord. Than Jesus said to her; Neither do I condemn you; go and sin no more. I am the light of the world; he that follows after me shall not walk in darkness, but shall have the light of life.

****

Jesus in the Treasury

Though I bear record of myself; my record is true; for I know from where I came and to where I go; but you cannot tell from where I have come from and where I go.

You judge after the flesh and I judge no man. And yet if I judge my judgment is true.

I am he that bears witness of myself, and the Father that sent me bears witness of me.

You neither know me or my Father which sent me; if you had known me than you would have known my Father also.

I go my way, and you shall seek me, and shall die in your sins; where I go you cannot come.

You are from beneath; I am from above; you are of this world; I am not of this world.

I said therefore to you, that you shall die in your sins; for if you believe not that I am he; you shall indeed die in your sins.

Then they said to him; Who are you? Even the same that I said to, you from the beginning.

I have many things to say and to judge of you; but he that sent me is true; and I speak to the world those things which I have heard of him.

When you have lifted up the Son of man, then you shall know that I am he and that I do nothing of myself; but as my Father has taught me, I speak those things.

And he that sent me is with me; the Father has not left me alone; for I always do those things which please him.

If you continue in my word then you are my disciples indeed. And you shall know the truth and the truth shall make you free.

Truly, truly I say to you, that he that commits sin is the servant of sin. And the servant abides not in the house forever, but the Son abides forever.

If the Son therefore shall make you free you shall be free indeed.

****

Christ and the Hypocrites

I know that you are Abraham's seed; but you seek to kill me, because my word has no place in you.

I speak that which I have seen with my Father; and you do that which you have seen with your father.

They said to him; Abraham is our father. He said; If you were Abraham's children, you would do the works of Abraham.

But now you seek to kill me, a man that has told you the truth, which I have heard of God; Abraham did not this.

You do the deeds of your father. If God were you father you would have loved me; for I proceeded forth and came from God; neither came I of myself but he sent me.

Why do you not understand my speech? Even because you cannot hear my words.

You are of your father the devil, and the lusts of your father you will do.

He was a murderer from the beginning and abode not in the truth, because there is no truth in him.

When he speaks a lie he speaks of his own; for he is a liar and the father of it.

And because I tell you the truth, you do not believe me. Which of you convinces me of sin? And if I say the truth why do you, not believe me?

He that is of God hears God's words; you therefore hear them not because you are not of God.

The Jews then said to him; We have well said that you are a Samaritan and you have a devil.

Jesus replied; I don't have a devil; but I honor my Father, and you do dishonor me.

And I seek not my own glory; there is one that seeks and judges. Truly I say to you; If a man keeps my sayings he shall not see death.

****

The Divine Christ

If I honor myself my honor is nothing; it is my Father which honors me; of whom you say that he is your God.

Yet you have not known him; but I know him; and if I should say that I know him not, I shall be a liar like you; but I know him and keep his sayings. Your Father Abraham rejoiced to see my day; and he saw it and was glad.

The Jews said to him; You are not fifty years old how have you seen Abraham? He said to them; Truly, before Abraham was, I am.

My Prayer..... May we never take for granted how great a salvation that you have bestowed upon us… Amen

****

The Blind Man Question

As Jesus passed by he took notice of a man who was blind from birth. His disciples asked him; Master, who did sin, his father or his mother that he was born blind?

Jesus said; Neither has this man sinned nor did his parents; but that the works of God should be made manifest in him.

I must work the works of him that sent me, while it is day; for the night comes when no man can work.

As long as I am in the world I am the light of the world. After he said this he spit on the ground and made clay of the spittle, and he anointed the eyes of the blind man with the clay.

And he said to him; Go and wash in the pool of Siloam. The man went and did as he had said and came again seeing.

Later the Jews argued with the healed man saying; Who is that healed you? And they referred to Christ as a sinner.

The man replied; If this man were not of God, he could do nothing. The Jews said to the man that he also was altogether a sinner and who was he to teach them. And they cast him out of their presence.

Later after Jesus heard what had happened to the man he found him and said to him; Do you believe in the Son of God?

And he answered saying; Who is he Lord that I might believe in him?

Jesus said; You have both seen him and it is he that talks with you. And he said, Lord I believe and worshipped him.

For judgment I have come into the world, that they which see not might see, and that they which see may be made blind.

Some of the Pharisees were near him, and hearing what he had said they asked him; Are we blind also?

Jesus answered saying; If you were blind you would have no sin; but now you say we see; therefore your sin remains.

****

The Good Shepard

Truly, truly I say to you, he that does not enter by the door into the sheepfold, but climbs up some other way, the same is a thief and a robber.

But he that enters in by the door is the Shepard of the sheep. To him the porter opens; and the sheep hear his voice; and he calls his own sheep by name, and leads them out.

And when he puts out his own sheep, he goes before them, and his sheep follow him, for they know his voice.

And a stranger they will not follow, but will flee from him; for they do not know the voice of strangers.

****

The Door

Truly, truly, I say to you; I am the door of the sheep. All that ever came before me are thieves and robbers; but the sheep did not hear them.

I am the door; by me if any man enter, he shall be saved, and shall go in and out and find pasture. The thief comes not but for to steal to kill and to destroy.

I have come that they may have life and that they may have it more abundantly.

I am the good shepard and the good shepard gives his life for the sheep.

But he that is a hireling and not the good shepard, whose own sheep they are not; sees the wolf coming, and leaves the sheep and flees. And the wolf catches them and scatters the sheep.

The hireling flees because he is a hireling and does not care for the sheep. I am the good shepard, and I know my sheep, and am known by them.

As the Father knows me, even so I know the Father; and I lay down my life for the sheep.

And other sheep I have, which are not of this fold; them also I must bring and they also shall hear my voice; and there shall be one fold and one shepard.

Therefore does my Father love me, because I lay down my life that I might take it again. No man takes it from me, but I lay it down of myself.

I have the power to lay it down and to take it again. This commandment I have received of my Father.

****

Christ's Divinity

I told you and you did not believe me. The works that I do in my Fathers name, they bear witness of me. But you believed not because you are not of my sheep, as I said to you.

My sheep hear my voice, and I know them, and they follow me.

And I give to them eternal life; and they shall never perish, neither shall any man pluck them out of my hand.

My Father which gave them to me; is greater than all; and no man is able to pluck them out of my Fathers hand. I and my Father are one.

****

The Jews Attempt to Stone Him

Many good works I have shown you from my Father; for which of those good works do you stone me? Is it not written in your law, I said you are gods?

If he called them gods, to whom the word of God came, and the scripture cannot be broken.

Do you say to him that the Father has sanctified, and sent into their world, you blaspheme, because I said I am the Son of God?

If I don't do the works of my Father than do not believe me. But if I do; even though you don't believe me; believe in the works; that you may know and believe that the Father is in me and I am in him.

****

The Resurrection of Lazarus

Mary came to the Lord saying that my brother whom you love is sick. This was the same Mary who had anointed Christ with oil and wiped his feet with her hair.

Jesus said; This sickness is not unto death, but for the glory of God, that the Son of God may be glorified thereby.

After hearing this he still waited two more days before saying to his disciples; Let us go into Judea again.

Are there not yet twelve hours in a day? If any man walks in the day he does not stumble, because he sees the light of this world.

But if a man walks at night, he stumbles, because there is no light in him. He then said; Our friend Lazarus is sleeping, but I am going that I may awaken him out of his sleep.

He then told them plainly; Lazarus is dead. And I am glad for your sakes that I was not there, to the intent that you may believe; nevertheless let us go to him.

Martha who was Mary's sister, when she had heard Christ was coming ran out to meet him, while Mary stayed at home.

Then Martha said; If you had been here he would not have died; nevertheless I know that whatever you ask of God he will give it to you. Jesus said; Your brother shall rise again.

I am the resurrection and the life; he that believes in me, though he were dead, yet he shall live again. And whoever lives and believes in me shall never die. Do you believe this?

A short time later he asked them where they had laid him. They took him to the grave which was a cave with a stone laid in front of it.

Jesus said to them; Take away the stone. Martha said to Jesus; By now his body stinks because he has been dead four days.

Jesus said; Did I not say to you, that if you would believe; you should see the glory of God.

With that Jesus lifted up his eyes and said; Father I thank you that you have heard me.

And I know that you hear me always; but because of the people which stand by I said it, that they may believe that you have sent me.

He then cried with a loud voice; Lazarus, come forth! And Lazarus came out of the tomb bound hand a foot in the graveclothes. Jesus said to them; Loose him and let him go.

My Prayer….. Lord May we always be mindful that the Father hears us as we pray… Amen

****

Mary's Anointing of Christ

After Lazarus had been raised from the dead, Jesus came to his house six days before the Passover. His sister Mary anointed the Lord with some very expensive ointment.

She also wiped his feet with her own hair. Than Judas; the one who would betray him said; This ointment could have been sold for much money and given to the poor.

Of course he did not care for the poor at all, but said this only out of greed for the lost money. Jesus said; Leave her alone; for the day of my burial she has saved this ointment.

For the poor you have always with you; but me you do not always have.

****

Christ Announces His Own Sufferings

The hour has come that the Son of man should be glorified. Truly, truly I say to you, unless a corn of wheat falls into the ground and die, it abides alone; but if it dies it will bring forth much fruit.

He that loves his life shall loose it; and he that hates his life in this world shall keep it to eternal life.

If any man serve me, let him follow me. And where I am, there shall my servant be also. If any man serves me; him will my Father honor.

Now is my soul troubled. And what shall I say, Father save me from this hour? But for this cause I came to this hour. Father glorify your name.

There came a great voice from heaven saying. I have glorified it and will glorify it again. Jesus said; This voice came not because of me; but for your sakes.

Now is the judgment of this world. Now shall the prince of this world be cast out. And if I be lifted up from the earth, I will draw all men unto me.

****

Christ the Light

Yet a little while longer is the light with you, walk while you have the light; unless darkness come upon you. For he that walks in darkness does not know where he is going.

While you have the light, believe in the light; that you may be children of the light.

****

Christ Rebukes the Rulers

He that believes in me; believes not in me but in him that sent me. And he that sees me sees him that sent me.

I have come into the world that whoever believes in me should not abide in darkness.

And if any man hears my words and believes not; I do not judge him; for I came not to judge the world but to save it.

He that rejects me and receives not my words, has one that will judge him; the word that I have spoken; the same will judge him in the last day.

For I have not spoken of myself; but the Father which sent me; he gave me a commandment, what I should say and what I should speak.

And I know that this commandment is life everlasting; whatever therefore I speak; even as the Father said to me, therefore I speak.

****

Christ Washes His Disciples Feet

As Christ began washing his disciple's feet; Peter said to him; Will you wash my feet Lord? And Jesus said; What I do you do not know; but you shall know from hereafter.

Peter said; you shall never wash my feet. Jesus said; If I do not wash you, you will have no part in me.

Then Peter said; Wash not only my feet but my hands and my head also.

Jesus said. He that is washed needs only to wash his feet, and is made clean everywhere; and you are clean but not all; This he said knowing that one would betray him.

Then he said to them; Do you know what I have done to you? You call me master and Lord and you say it well for so I am.

If I then your Lord and master have washed your feet; you also should wash one another's feet. For I have given you an example that as I have done you should do also.

Truly, truly I say to you; that the servant is not greater than his lord; neither is he that is sent greater than him that sent him. If you know these things happy are you if you do them.

I speak not of you all; I know whom I have chosen; but that the scripture may be fulfilled; he that eats bread with me has lifted up his heal against me.

Now I tell you before it comes to pass; that when it comes to pass, you may believe that I am he.

Truly, truly I say to you, whoever receives him whom I send receives me also; and he that receives me receives him that sent me.

Truly I say to you that one of you shall betray me. His disciples argued among themselves as to who it would be.

Then Jesus said; It is he to whom I shall give the sop after I have dipped it. He gave it to Judas Iscariot. After this Satan entered into Judas. Jesus said to him; What you must do, do it quickly.

Jesus said; Now is the Son of man glorified, and God is glorified in him.

If God be glorified in him, God shall also glorify him in himself, and shall straightway glorify him.

Little children; yet a little while am I with you.

You shall seek me; and as I said to the Jews; where I go you cannot come; so now I say it to you.

A new commandment I have given you that you, love one another; as I have loved you, that you also love one another.

By this shall men know that you are my disciples; if you have love one for another.

Then Peter said to him; Where are you going? Jesus said to him; Where I am going you cannot follow me now; but you shall follow me afterwards.

Peter said; Why can I not follow you now? I will lay down my life for you. Jesus said; Will you lay your life down? Before the cock crows you shall deny me three times.

****

Christ the Comforter

Let not your heart be troubled; you believe in God believe also in me. In my Fathers house there are many mansions; if it was not so I would have told you.

I am going to prepare a place for you. And if I go to prepare a place for you, I will come again to receive you unto myself; that where I am you may be also.

And where I am going you know and the way you also know.

I am the way the truth and the life, no man comes to the Father but by me. If you had known me you would have known my Father also. And from this time forward you have both known him and seen him.

Phillip than said to him; Show us the Father and it will be enough.

Jesus said; Have I been such a long time with you, and yet you do not know me Phillip?

He that has seen me has seen the Father; and how do you say then show us the Father?

Do you not believe that I am in the Father and that the Father is in me?

The words that I speak to you I speak not of my self; but the Father that dwells in me he does the works.

Believe me that I am in the Father and the Father is in me; or else believe me for the very works sake.

Truly I say to you, he that believes in me; the works that I do he shall do also; and greater works shall he do also; because I go to the Father.

And whatsoever you ask in my name that shall I do; that the Father may be glorified in the Son. If you ask anything in my name I will do it.

If you love me keep my commandments. And I will pray to the Father and he shall give you another Comforter that he may abide with you forever.

Even the Spirit of truth that the world cannot receive; because it sees him not, neither do they know him. But you know him for he dwells within you and shall be in you.

I will not leave you comfortless; I will come to you. Yet a little while and the world will see me no more; but you see me; and because I live you shall live also.

At that day you shall know that I am in the Father and you are in me and I am in you.

He that has my commandments and keeps them; he it is that loves me; and he that loves me shall be loved of my Father, and I will love him and will manifest myself to him.

He that loves me not keeps not my sayings; and the word which you hear is not mine; but the Fathers who sent me.

These things have I spoken to you being yet present with you.

But the Comforter which is the Holy Ghost, who the Father will send in my name, he shall teach you all things, and bring all things to your remembrance, whatever I have said to you.

Peace I leave with you, my peace I give to you; not as the world gives it do I give it to you. Let not your heart be troubled neither let it be afraid.

You have heard how I say to you, I go away, and will come again to you. If you loved me you would rejoice, because I said I go to the Father; for my Father is greater than I am.

And know I have told you before it comes to pass, that when it has come to pass you may believe.

Hereafter I will not talk much with you; for the prince of this world is coming and he has nothing in me.

But that the world may know that I love the Father; and as the Father gave me a commandment; even so I do; Arise lets us go where we must.

My Prayer….. May we continually follow you and your ways all the days of our lives until you come again Lord Jesus… Amen

****

Christ the Vine

I am the true vine and my Father is the husbandman. Every branch in me that bears no fruit he takes it away; and every branch that bears fruit he prunes it, that it may bring forth more fruit.

Now you are clean through the word which I have spoken to you. Abide in me and I in you.

As the branch cannot bear fruit of itself, unless it abides in the vine; no more can you unless you abide in me.

I am them vine you are the branches, he that abides in me and I in him, the same brings forth much fruit; for without me you can do nothing.

If a man does not abide in me he his cast out as a branch and withers away; and men gather them up and they are cast into the fire to be burned.

If you abide in me, and my words abide in you, you shall ask what you will and it shall be done for you. In this is my Father glorified; that you should bear much fruit; so shall you be my disciples.

As the Father has loved me; so also I have loved you; continue you in my love.

If you keep my commandments you shall abide in my love; even as I have kept my Fathers commandments and abide in his love.

These things have I spoken to you; that my joy may remain in you, and that you joy may remain full. This is my commandment; that you should love one another as I have loved you.

Greater love has no man than this; that he should lay down his life for his friends. You are my friends if you do whatever I command you to do.

From hereon I call you not servants; for the servant does not know what his lord does; but I have called you friends; for all things that I have heard of my Father I have made known to you.

You have not chosen me but I have chosen you, and ordained you, that you should go forth and bear much fruit, and that your fruit should remain.

That whatever you ask of the Father in my name he may give it to you.

These things I command you; that you should love one another. If the world hates you; know that it hated me before it hated you.

If you were of the world, the world would love its own; but because you are not of the world; but I have chosen you out of the world, therefore the world hates you.

Remember the word that I said to you; the servant is not greater than his lord. If they have persecuted me; they will also persecute you.

If they have kept my saying they will keep yours also.

But all these things they will do to you for my namesake, because they do not know him that sent me.

If I had not come and spoken to them they had no sin; but now they have no cloak to hide behind for their sin. He that hates me hates my Father also.

If I had not done among them the works which no other man did, they had not had sin; but now they have both seen and hated both me and my Father.

But this comes to pass that the word might be fulfilled that is written in their law; that they hated me without a cause.

But when the Comforter has come that I will send to you from my Father, even the Spirit of Truth, which proceeds from my Father, he shall testify of me.

And you shall also bear witness for you have been with me from the beginning.

****

The Glory of Christ

These things have I spoken to you that you should not be offended. They shall put you out of the synagogues.

Yes the time is coming that whoever kills you will think he is doing God a service.

And these things will they do to you because they have not known the Father or me.

But these things have I told you; that when the time shall come; that you may remember that I told you of them.

And these things I said to you at the beginning because I was with you.

But Now I am going my way to him that sent me; and none of you asks me; where are you going? But because I have said these things to you; sorrow has filled your heart.

Nevertheless I tell you the truth; it is expedient for you that I go away; for if I do not go away the Comforter will not come for you; but if I depart, I will send him to you.

And when he has come; he will reprove the world of sin, and of righteousness and of judgment. Of sin because they believe not in me.

Of righteousness because I go to my Father and you will see me no more. Of judgment because the prince of this world is judged.

I have yet many things to say to you; but you cannot bare them now.

Howbeit, when he the Spirit of truth, has come, he will guide you in all truth; for he shall not speak of himself; but whatever he shall hear; that shall he speak; and he will show you things to come.

He shall glorify me; for he shall receive of mine and shall show it to you.

All things that then Father has are mine; therefore I said to you; that I shall take of mine and show it to you. A little while and you shall not see me; and again a little while and you shall see me, because I am going to the Father.

****

The Disciples are Puzzled

Do you speak among your selves as to what I said; A little while and you shall not see me; and again a little while and you shall see me?

Truly, truly I say to you; that you shall weep and lament; but the world shall rejoice and you shall be sorrowful; but you sorrow shall be turned to joy.

A woman when she is in labor has sorrow; because her hour has come; but as soon as she has delivered the child she remembers no more the anguish, for the joy that a man is born into the world.

And now you therefore have sorrow; but I will see you again and your heart shall rejoice, and your joy can no man take from you. And in that day you shall ask me nothing.

Truly, truly I say to you; whatever you shall ask the Father in my name, he will give it to you. Up until now you have asked nothing in my name; ask and you shall receive that your joy may be full.

These things I have spoken to you in proverbs; but the time comes when I shall no longer speak to you in proverbs, but I will show you plainly of the Father.

At that time you shall ask in my name; and I say not to you that I will pray to the Father for you. For the Father himself loves you because you loved me, and have believed that I came out from God.

I came forth from the Father; and have come into the world; and again, I leave the world and go again to the Father.

Do you now believe? Behold the hour has come, yes, and now is, that you shall be scattered, every man to his own, and you shall leave me alone. And yet I am not alone because the Father is with me.

These things I have spoken to you; that in me you may have peace. In the world you shall have tribulation. But be of good cheer; I have overcome the world.

****

Christ's Prayer to the Father

Father the hour has come, glorify your Son, that your Son may also glorify you. As you have given him power over all flesh, that he should give eternal life to as many as you have given him.

And this is life eternal; that they might know you; the only eternal true God, and Jesus Christ whom you have sent. I have glorified you on the earth, and I have finished the work which you gave me to do.

And now Father, glorify me with thine own self and with the glory which I had with you before the world was.

I have manifested your name with the men which you gave me out of the world; yours they were and you gave them to me, and they have kept your word.

Not they have known that all things. Whatever you have given me, are of you. For I have given to them the words which you gave me, and they have received them, and have known surely that I came out from you, and they have believed that you did send me.

I pray for them; I pray not for the world, but for them which you have given me; for they are yours. And all mine are yours and yours are mine; and I am glorified in them.

And now I am no more in the world; but these are in the world, and I come to you. Holy Father; keep through your own name those that you have given me, that they may be one as we are.

While I was with them in the world I kept them in your name; those that you gave me I have kept, and none of them is lost accept the son of perdition; that the scripture might be fulfilled.

And now I come to you; and these things that I have fulfilled in the world; that they might have my joy fulfilled in themselves.

I have given them your word; and the world has hated them, because they are not of the world even as I am not of the world.

I pray not that you should take them out of the world but that you should keep them from evil. They are not of the world even as I am not of the world.

Sanctify them through your truth; your word is truth. As you have sent me into the world; even so I have sent them into the world.

And for their sakes I sanctify myself, that they also may be sanctified through the truth. Neither do I pray for these alone; but for them also which shall believe in me by their words.

That they all may be one; as you Father are in me and I am in you; that they also may be one in us; that the world may believe that you have sent me.

And the glory which you have given to me; I have given to them; that they may be one as we are one. I in them and you in me; that they may be made perfect in one; and that the world may know that you have sent me.

And the glory which you gave me; I have given to them; that they may be one even as we are one.

I in them and you in me, that they may be made perfect in one; and that the world may know that you have sent me, and have loved them, as you have loved me.

Father I will that they also which you have given me, be with me where I am; that they may behold my glory; which you give to me; for you loved me before the foundation of the world.

Oh righteous Father, the world has not known you; but I have known you; and these have known you which you have sent me. And I have declared to them your name, and will declare it; that the love with which you have loved me may be in them, and I in them.

****

Judas Betrays Christ

As Judas and those that he had brought with him approached Jesus he said to them; Whom do you seek? They answered and said to him; Jesus of Nazareth. Then the Lord said to them; I am he.

And as soon as he had said this they moved backward and fell upon the ground. Then Jesus again said to them; Whom do you seek. And they again said; Jesus of Nazareth.

He then said; I have told you that I am he; if therefore you seek me then let these others go their way. Then Simon Peter took his sword and cut off the ear of one of the men.

Jesus then said to Peter; Put your sword in its sheath; the cup which my Father has given me; shall I not drink it?

****

The Examination by the High Priest

Christ was asked by the priest about his disciples and of his doctrine. Jesus said; I spoke openly in the world; teaching always in the synagogue; and in the temple where the Jews always resort; and in secret have I said nothing.

Why do you ask me what are my teachings? Ask them that heard me, what I have said to them; behold they know what I said.

And when he had said this one of the officers struck him in the face. Jesus then said; If I have spoken evil then bear witness of the evil; but if well than why have you hit me?

****

Christ is Brought Before Pilate

Pilate entered the judgment hall again and said to the Lord; Are you the King of the Jews? Jesus said to him; Do you say this thing of yourself or did others say it to you about me?

Then Pilate said; Your own people and chief priests have delivered you to me; what have you done? Jesus answered; My kingdom is not of this world; if it were then my servants would fight, that I should not be delivered to the Jews; but now is my kingdom not from here.

Pilate then said to him; Then are you a king? Jesus said; You say that I am king. To his end was I born and for this cause I came into the world, that I should bear witness to the truth. Everyone that is of the truth hears my voice.

****

Pilate Examines Jesus Further

Later Pilate said to him; Why don't you speak to me? Do you not know that I have then power to crucify you or to set you free?

Christ said; You could have no power at all against me, except it was given to you from above; therefore he that delivered me to you has the greater sin.

****

At the Crucifixion

While on the cross, Jesus looked down on Mary and said to her; Woman, Behold your son! Then he said to the disciple who was with her; Behold your mother!

A short time later that the scripture might be fulfilled he said; I thirst. After this Christ said; It is finished. And he bowed his head and gave up the ghost.

****

After the Burial

Mary Magdalene stood outside of the tomb weeping, and as she was weeping she stooped down and looked inside of the tomb and saw two angels sitting where Jesus body had been laid.

They said to her; why are you weeping? She said to them; Because they have taken away the body of my Lord. And when she had finished saying this she turned around, and saw Jesus standing there, only she did not know that it was him.

Jesus said to her; Woman, why are you weeping? Whom do you seek? She then supposing him to be the gardener said to him; Have you taken him from here?

And if so where have you laid him that I may go see him? With this he said to her; Mary. She turned and said to him, Rabboni, which is to say Master.

He then said to her; Do not touch me for I have not yet ascended to my Father; but go to my brethren and say to them, that I ascend to my Father and to your Father; and to my God and to your God.

Later that same day where the doors were shut up for fear where the disciples were staying, Jesus came and stood in their midst and said to them; Peace be unto you.

And when he had thus said this he showed them his hands and his side and they were glad.

Then he said to them; peace be unto you; as my Father has sent me, even so I send you.

Having said this he breathed on them and said; Receive you the Holy Ghost. Whosever's sins you remit, they are remitted of them; and whosever's sins you retain, they are retained of them.

Eight days after this Jesus returned to the disciples, and this time Thomas was with them. He said; Peace be unto you.

Then he said to Thomas; Reach here with you finger, and behold my hands; and reach out with your hand and put it into my side; and be not faithless but believing.

Then Thomas said to him; My Lord and my God. Jesus said to him; Thomas, because you have seen me you have believed; blessed are they that have not seen and yet believe.

Yet again at a later date, Christ appears again to seven of the disciples as they were fishing. He stood on the shore and said to them; Children do you have any meat?

And they said to him no. Again not knowing that it was him. Jesus said too them; Cast your net on the right side of the ship and you shall find them.

Upon doing so their nets were filled to the bursting and Peter said; It is the Lord, and jumped into the water to swim to shore.

When they came to shore they saw Jesus, and a fire going upon which fish were laid. He said to them; Bring the fish which you have now caught.

Then he said to them, come and dine. After eating Jesus said to Simon Peter; Simon son of Jonas, do you love me more than these? And he said yes.

Then Jesus said feed my sheep. Then a second time he said to Peter; Simon, son of Jonas, do you love me?

And he said again; Yes Lord, you know that I love you. Again he said to him, feed my sheep. And yet a third time he said to Peter; Simon, do you love me?

And again Peter said to him, Lord you know all things, yes I love you. And again Jesus said to him, feed my sheep.

Truly, truly I say to you, that when you were young you girded yourself and walked wherever you would; but when you shall be old, you shall stretch forth your hands and another shall gird you and carry you where you would not go.

This he spoke knowing the death that he would face, crucifixion. Then he said to him; follow me. Then Peter turned and saw the apostle which Jesus loved following them and he said to Christ; What shall this man do?

Jesus said; If it is my will that he should wait until I come, what is that to you? Follow me!

My Prayer….. Blessed are they who have believed and not seen Lord Jesus. May I be ever vigilant and faithful until the day of my death… Amen

The Acts of the Apostles

The Commission

After his resurrection from the dead, and having appeared to and assembled with the disciples, he told them not to leave Jerusalem.

And he said to them: Wait for, the promise of the Father which he said, you have heard from me. They then said to him; Lord will you at this time restore again the kingdom to Israel?

He said; It is not for you to know the times or the seasons, which the Father has put in his own power. But you shall receive power after that the Holy Ghost has come upon you; and you shall be witnesses to me both in Jerusalem and in all Judea, and in Samaria, and to the uttermost parts of the earth.

****

Saul's Conversion

As Saul journeyed on the road to Dasmascus, having the authority to imprison the disciples of Christ, there shone about him a light from heaven.

Jesus said to him; Saul, Saul, why do you persecute me? And Saul said; Who are you Lord? I am Jesus whom you persecute; it is hard for you to kick against the pricks.

Trembling with fear he said to Jesus; Lord what would you have me to do? Jesus said; Arise and go into the city, and it shall be told to you what you must do.

And Saul got up blinded, and was led by the hand by those that were with him three days journey into Damascus.

And in Damascus there was a certain disciple named Ananias, who the Lord came to in a vision.

He said; Ananias, arise and go into the street which is called Straight, and enquire in the house of Judas for a man named Saul of Tarsus; for behold he is praying.

And he has seen in a vision a man named Ananias coming in, and putting his hand on him, that he might receive his sight.

Ananias said to the Lord; I have heard much evil about this man, how he has done much bad against the saints at Jerusalem.

Jesus said to Ananias; Go your way for he is a chosen vessel for me, to bear my name before the Gentiles, and kings, and the children of Israel.

For I will show him how many great things he must suffer for my namesake.

****

Peters Call to Caesarea

Peter having been sent by the Lord to the Gentiles, after having returned was being contended with by the Jewish disciples as to why he went to the Gentiles. And as he was explaining to them the vision he had seen. And why he had done what he did.

He then said to them, that while he spoke to the Gentiles, that the Holy Ghost fell on them as it had on the disciples.

He then remembered what Jesus spoke saying; John indeed baptized with water; but you shall be baptized with the Holy Ghost.

Peter than said who am I to contend with God giving to them then same gift he gave to us.

****

Paul's Ministerial Calling

Paul after having left Athens and gone to Corinth, met and stayed with Aquila and his wife Priscilla for the three of them were all tentmakers by trade.

And while there Paul was in the synagogue every Sabbath persuading both the Jews and the Greeks that Jesus was the Christ.

And when the Jews opposed themselves and blasphemed, Paul shook the dust from his clothing and said to them;

Your blood be on your own heads, I am clean, from hereon I will go to the Gentiles.

And when he departed from there he entered into the house of Justus, who was a man that worshipped God and whose house was next to the synagogue.

And Chrispus, who was the chief ruler on the synagogue, believed in the Lord with his whole family. And many people in Corinth believed and were baptized.

Then the Lord spoke to Paul in a night vision saying; Be not afraid; but speak, and hold not your peace; For I am with you and no man shall set on you to hurt you; for I have much people in this city.

****

Paul is Seized by a Mob in Jerusalem

Paul was in Jerusalem preaching the gospel, and a mob set upon him seeking to kill him. The Roman soldiers seeing what was happening grabbed Paul and questioned him as to what was going on.

During this questioning Paul told them that he was a Roman citizen by birth which troubled the soldiers for you could not hold a Roman citizen without a cause.

He then asked if he could address the crowd and they allowed him to do so.

He told them of his journey to Damascus where the Lord shone a light upon him and he was blinded, the Lord saying to him; Saul, Saul, why do you persecute me?

And he said Lord who are you; And a voice said to him; I am Jesus of Nazareth whom you persecute. He continued saying that they who were with him saw the light but did not hear the voice.

He then told them that he said; What shall I do Lord? And the Lord said to me; Arise and go to Damascus; and there it shall be told to you of all the things that you are to do.

He then told of Ananias setting his hands on him and how after this he was able to see again. Ananias then told him; The God of our fathers has chosen you that you should know his will, and see the Just One, and should hear the voice of his mouth.

And you shall be a witness unto all men of what you have seen and heard.

And after this I was baptized for the washing away of my sins and the Lord appeared to me saying; Make haste, and get quickly out of Jerusalem; for they will not receive your testimony concerning me.

Later it was determined that Paul should be taken to Rome and that his case should be heard there.

The night following this the Lord stood by his side and said to Paul; Be of good cheer Paul; for as you have testified of me in Jerusalem, so must you bear witness of me also in Rome.

So Paul is brought before King Agrippa. And the king tells him that he is permitted to speak for himself. Paul again testifies of his conversion saying; At midday oh king, I saw in the way a light from heaven, above the brightness of the sun shining round about me and them that journeyed with me.

And when we had all fallen to the ground, I heard a voice saying in the Hebrew tongue; Saul Saul, why do you persecute me? It is hard for you to kick against the pricks. And when I said who are you Lord? The voice said to me; Rise and stand upon your feet.

For I have appeared to you for this purpose, to make of you both a minister and a witness, both of these things which you have seen, and of those things which shall appear to you; Delivering you from the people, and from the Gentiles, unto whom I now send you.

To open their eyes and to turn them from darkness to light, and from the power of Satan to God, that they may receive the forgiveness of sins, and an inheritance among them which are sanctified by faith which is in me.

My Prayer….. Lord may we all have the boldness which was instilled in Paul by your Spirit to testify of your goodness and your salvation to all people… Amen

The Revelation of Saint John

The Revelation of Saint John

I am the Alpha and the Omega, the beginning and the ending, says the Lord, which is, and which was, and which is to come, the Almighty.

This is the account of Saint Johns vision while imprisoned on the isle of Patmos. Included are only the portions of the vision where the Lord Jesus was speaking to him.

I John who also am your brother, and companion in tribulation, and in the kingdom and patience of Jesus Christ, was in the isle that is called Patmos, because of my testimony pertaining to the word of God and Jesus Christ.

I was in the Spirit on the Lord's day, and heard behind me a great voice, as of a mighty trumpet.

The voice said to me. I am Alpha and Omega, the first and the last, and what you see, write in a book, and send it to the seven churches which are in Asia; to Ephesus, and to Smyrna, and to Pergamos, and to Thyatira, and to Sardis, and to Philadelphia, and to Laodicea.

John then said he turned to see the voice that spoke to him. And having turned he saw seven golden candlesticks; And in the middle of the seven candlesticks, one who looked like the Son of Man, clothed with a garment down to his feet and wrapped about his loins with a golden girdle.

His head and his hair were white like wool, as white as snow; and his eyes were as flaming fire.

And his feet were like fine brass, as if they were burning in a furnace; and his voice was as the sound of many waters.

And he had in his right hand seven stars, and out of his mouth went a sharp two edged sword; and his appearance was as the sun shining in its strength.

And when I saw him I fell at his feet as though I was dead. And he laid his right hand upon me and spoke to me.

Fear not, I am the first and the last; I am he that lived and was dead; and behold I am alive forever more, Amen; and have the keys of hell and of death.

Write down the things which you have seen, and the things which are, and the things which shall be hereafter; the mystery of the seven stars which you saw in my right hand, and the seven golden candlesticks.

The seven stars are the angels of the seven churches; and the seven candlesticks which you saw are the seven churches.

****

Christ Addresses the Churches

Unto the angel of the church at Ephesus write this; These things says he that holds the seven stars in his right hand, who walks in the midst of the seven golden candlesticks.

I know your works and your labor, and your patience, and how you cannot bear those that are evil; and you have tried them which say that they are apostles, and are not, and have found them to be liars.

And you have born and have had patience, and for my namesake you have labored much and have not fainted.

Nevertheless I have somewhat against you, because you have left your first love.

Remember therefore the height from which you have fallen, and repent, and do your first works; or else I will come to you quickly, and remove your candlestick out of its place, unless you repent.

But this you have, that you hate the deeds of the Nicolaitanes, which I also hate.

He that has an ear let him hear what the Spirit says to the churches; To him that overcomes I will allow him to eat of the tree of life, which is in the midst of the paradise of God.

And to the angel in the church of Smyrna write this; These things says the first and the last; he which was dead and is alive.

I know your works and tribulation, and poverty, but you are rich, and I know the blasphemy of those who say that they are Jews, and are not, but are of the synagogue of Satan.

Fear none of those things which you shall suffer; behold the devil shall cast some of you into prison and you shall be tried; and you shall have tribulation for ten days.

Be faithful unto death and I will give you a crown of life; He that has an ear, let him listen to what the Spirit says to the churches. He that overcomes shall not be hurt of the second death.

And to the angel of the church at Pergamos write this; These things says he that has the sharp sword with two edges.

I know your works and where you dwell; even where Satan's seat is; and that you hold fast to my name, and have not denied my faith, even in those days when Antipas was my faithful martyr, who was slain among you where Satan dwells.

But I have a few things against you, because you have there those who hold to the doctrine of Balaam, who taught Balac to put a stumbling block before the children of Israel.

To eat such things that had been sacrificed to idols, and to commit fornication. So also do you have those who hold on to the doctrine of the Nicolaitines which thing I hate.

Repent or else I will come quickly, and fight against them with the sword of my mouth. He that has an ear let him hear what the Spirit says to the churches.

To him that overcomes I will give to eat of the hidden manna, and I will give to him a white stone, and on the stone a new name will be written, which no man will know except him to whom it is given.

And to the angel of the church at Thyatira write this; these things says the Son of God, whose eyes are like a flaming fire, and whose feet are like fine brass.

I know your works and charity, and service, and faith, and your patience, and works, and the last to be greater than the first. Not withstanding I have a few things against you.

Because you allow that woman Jezebel, who calls herself a prophetess, to teach and seduce my servants to commit fornication, and to eat things sacrificed to idols.

And I gave her space to repent of her fornication; and she repented not. Behold I will cast her into a bed, and those that commit adultery with her into a great tribulation, unless they repent of their deeds.

And I will kill her children with death; and all the churches will know that I am he who searches the reins and hearts; and I will give to every one of you according to your works.

But to you I say, and to the rest of Thyatira, as many as have not this doctrine, and who have not known the depths of Satan, as they speak; I will put upon you no other burden.

But that which you have already hold on fast to; until I come. And to him that overcomes and keeps my works to the end, to him I will give power over the nations. And he shall rule them with a rod of iron.

As the vessels of a potter, shall they be broken into shivers; even as I have received of my Father. And I will give to him the morning star. He that has an ear let him hear what the Spirit says to the churches.

And to the angel of the church at Sardis write this; These things says he that has the seven Spirits of God, and the seven stars; I know your works, and that you have a name, and that you live but are dead.

Be watchful and strengthen the things which remain, that are ready to die; for I have not found your works perfect before God.

Remember therefore what you have received and heard, and hold fast and repent. If you shall not watch, I will come on you as a thief. And you shall not know what hour I shall come upon you.

You have a few names even in Sardis that have not defiled their garments; and they shall walk with me in white; for they are worthy.

He that overcomes the same shall be clothed in white garments; and I will not blot his name out of the book of life; but will confess his name before my Father, and before his angels in heaven.

He that has an ear let him hear what the Spirit says unto the churches. And to the angel of the church in Philadelphia write this; these things say he that is holy, he that is true.

He that has the key of David, he that opens and no man shuts; and shuts and no man opens. I know your works; and behold I have set before you an open door; and no man can shut it.

Behold you have a little strength, and have kept my word and have not denied my name.

Behold I will make them of the synagogue of Satan, which say they are Jews, and are not, but do lie; behold I will make them to come and worship before your feet; and to know that I have loved you.

Because you have kept the word of my patience, I also will keep you from the hour of temptation, which shall come upon the entire world, to try them which dwell upon the earth.

Behold I come quickly; hold on fast to that which you have; let no man take your crown. Him that overcomes I will make a pillar in the temple of my God, and he shall go no more out.

And I will write upon him the name of my God, and the name of the city of my God, which is New Jerusalem, which comes down out of heaven from my God; and I will write upon him a new name.

He that has an ear let him hear what the Spirit says to the churches.

And to the angel of the church of the Laodiceans write this; These things say the Amen; the faithful and true witness, the beginning of the creation of God.

I know your works that you are neither cold nor hot. So then because you are lukewarm and neither cold nor hot I will spew you, out of my mouth.

Because you say I am rich and increased with goods, and have need of nothing; and you do not know that you are wretched, and miserable, and poor, and blind, and naked.

I counsel you to buy from me; gold tried in the fire; that you may be rich, and white garments, that you may be clothed, and that the shame of your nakedness not appear; and to anoint your eyes with eyesalve; that you may indeed see.

As many as I love, I rebuke and chasten; be zealous therefore and repent.

Behold I stand at the door and knock; if any man hears my voice and opens the door; I will come in and eat with him and he with me.

To him that overcomes will I grant to sit with me in my throne, even as I also overcame and have set down with my Father in his throne. He that has an ear let him hear what the Spirit says to the churches.

My Prayer….. May we consider Lord where we stand as individuals as we read this address to the churches. Not esteeming ourselves higher than we ought to, considering our brethren and humbling ourselves before your feet, unless we also should be caught in the snares of the devil. Help us Lord Jesus to live holy lives even as you are holy and have instructed us to do so… Amen

****

The Last Invitation

And, behold, I come quickly; and my reward is with me, to give to every man according as his work shall be. I am the Alpha and the Omega, the beginning and the end, the first and the last.

Then John writes this; Blessed are they that do his commandments that they may have then right to eat of the tree of life, and may enter through the gates of the city of God.

For outside of the gates are dogs, and sorcerers, and whoremongers, and murderers, and idolaters, and whoever loves to tell a lie. I Jesus have sent my angel to testify to you these things in the churches.

I am the root and the offspring of David, and the bright and morning star. John ends with this admonition; The Spirit and the bride say come.

And let him who is thirsty come. And let him that hears say come. And whoever will, let him take the water of life freely.

For I testify to every man that hears the words of the prophecy of this book, if any man should add to the things of this book; God shall add to him of the plagues written in this book.

And if any man shall take away from the words of this book of prophecy, God shall take away his part out of the book of life, and out of the holy city, and from the things which are written in this book. He who testifies of these things says; Surely, I come quickly. Amen

This is Christ's last biblical statement; Surely I am coming quickly. Amen. Even so come Lord Jesus. The grace of our Lord Jesus Christ be with you all. Amen.

Who is Jesus Christ According to the Scriptures?

Jesus the Living Word

John chapter 1 vs. 1-14

In the beginning was the Word, and the Word was with God, and the Word was God. The same was in the beginning with God.

All things were made by him; and without him was not anything made that was made. In him was life; and the life was the light of men. And the light shined in darkness and the darkness comprehended it not.

There was a man sent from God, whose name was John. The same came as a witness; to bear witness to the Light, that all men through him might believe. He, John, was not that light but was sent to bear witness of that light.

That he was the true light which lights every man that comes into the world. He was in the world, and the world was made by him, and the world knew him not.

He came to his own, and his own did not receive him. But to as many as did receive him, to them he gave the power to become the sons of God, even to those who believed in his name.

Which were born not of blood, nor by the will of the flesh, nor by the will of man, but by God. And the Word became flesh and dwelt among us, and we beheld his glory, the glory of the only begotten Son of the Father, the fullness of grace and truth.

Revelation chapter 19 vs. 11-16

And I saw heaven opened, and behold a white horse; and he that sat upon him was called Faithful and True, and in righteousness does he judge and make war.

His eyes were as a flame of fire, and on his head were many crowns, and he had a name written which no man new except himself. And he was clothed with a vesture that was dipped in blood; and his name is called; The Word of God.

And all the armies which were in heaven followed him upon white horses clothed in fine linens, which were white and clean.

And out of his mouth went a sharp sword, with which he will smite the nations; and he shall rule them with a rod of iron; and he treads the winepress of the fierceness and wrath of Almighty God.

And he has on his vesture and on his thigh a name written, King of Kings and Lord of Lords.

1 John chapter 5 vs. 7

For there are three that bear record in heaven, the Father, the Word, and the Holy Ghost; and these three are one.

And there are three that bear witness on the earth, the Spirit, and the water, and the blood; and these three agree in one.

If we receive the witness of men, the witness of God is greater; for this is the witness of God which he has testified of his Son.

He that believes in the son of God has this witness in himself, he that believes not God has made him a liar; because he believes not the record which God gave of his son.

And this is that record, that God has given to us eternal life, an this life is in his Son. He that has the Son has life, and he that has not the Son of God has not life.

****

The Word in Our Lives

1 John chapter 2 vs. 4-6

He that says, I know him, and does not keep his commandments, is a liar, and the truth is not in him.

But whoever keeps his word, in him truly is the love of God perfected; by this we know that we are in him. He that says he abides in him, should himself also walk as he walked.

James chapter 1 vs. 21-22

Therefore put aside all filthiness and naughtiness, and receive with meekness the engrafted word, which is able also to save your souls. But be you doers of the word and not hearers only, deceiving your own souls.

Colossians chapter 3 vs. 14-17

And above all these things put on charity, which is the bond of perfectness. And let the peace of God rule in your hearts, to which also you are called in one body; and be thankful.

Let the word of God dwell in you richly in all wisdom; teaching and admonishing one another in psalms and hymns and spiritual songs, singing with grace in your hearts to the Lord.

Acts chapter 13 vs. 26-30

Men and bretheren, children of the stock of Abraham, and whoever among you fears God, to you is the word of this salvation sent.

For those that dwell at Jerusalem, and their rulers, because they did not know him, nor the voices of the prophets which are read every Sabbath day, they have fulfilled them in condemning him.

And though they found no cause of death in him, yet they asked Pilate that he should be slain. And when they had fulfilled all that was written of him, they took him down from the cross and laid him in a sepulcher. But God raised him from the dead.

John chapter 1 vs. 10-14

He was in the world and the world was made by him, and the world knew him not. He came to his own and his own received him not.

But as many as did receive him, to them he gave the power to become the sons of God, even to them that believe in his name. Which were born not of blood, nor by the will of the flesh, nor of the will of man, but by God.

And the Word of God was made flesh and dwelled among us, and we beheld his glory, the glory as of the only begotten Son of the Father, full of grace and truth.

Old Testament Prophecies of Jesus Christ and the New Testament Fulfillment

The Seed of a Woman

Genesis 3 vs. 15

And I will put enmity between you and the woman, and between your seed and her seed; it shall bruise your head, and you shall bruise his heel.

Galatians 4 vs. 4

But when the fullness of the time had come, God sent forth his son, made of a woman, made under the law.

****

Promised to Come from the Seed of Abraham

Genesis 18 vs. 18

Seeing that Abraham shall surely become a great and mighty nation and all the nations of the earth shall be blessed in him.

Acts 3 vs. 25

You are the children of the prophets, and of the covenant which God made with our fathers, saying unto Abraham, And to your seed shall all the kindred's of the earth be blessed.

****

Promised to Come from the Seed of Isaac

Genesis 17 vs. 19

And God said, Sarah thy wife shall bear you a son indeed; and you shall call his name Isaac; and I will establish my covenant with him for an everlasting covenant, and with his seed after him.

Matthew 1 vs. 2

Abraham begat Isaac, and Isaac begat Jacob; and Jacob begat Judas and his brethren.

****

Promised to Come from the Seed of Jacob

Numbers 24 vs. 17

I shall see him, but not now; I shall behold him; but not near; there shall come a Star out of Jacob, and a Scepter shall rise out of Israel, and shall smite the corners of Moab, and destroy the children of Sheth.

Luke 3 vs. 34

Which was the son of Jacob; who was the son of Isaac; who was the son of Abraham; who was the son of Thara; which was the son of Nachor?

****

A Descendant of the Tribe of Judah

Genesis 49 vs. 10

The scepter shall not depart from Judah, or a lawgiver from between his feet, until Shiloh comes; and unto him shall the gathering of the people be.

Luke 3 vs. 33

Which was the son of Amindab; which was the son of Aram; which was the son of Esrom; which was the son of Phares; which was the son of Judah.

****

To Be Heir of the Throne of David

Isaiah 9 vs. 7

Of the increase of his government and his peace there shall be no end, upon the throne of David, and upon his kingdom, to order it, and to establish it with justice and judgment from hence forth even forever. The zeal of the Lord of hosts will perform this.

Matthew 1 vs. 1

The book of the generations of Jesus Christ, the son of David, the son of Abraham.

****

His Place of Birth

Micah 5 vs. 2

But thou, Bethlehem Ephratah, though you be little among the thousands of Judah, yet out of you shall he come forth unto me that is to be ruler in Israel; whose goings forth have been from old and from everlasting.

Matthew 2 vs. 1

Now when Jesus was born in Bethlehem of Judea in the days of Herod the king, behold there came wise men from the east to Jerusalem.

****

His Time of Birth

Daniel 9 vs. 25

Know therefore and understand, that from the going forth of the commandment to restore and to rebuild Jerusalem unto the Messiah the prince shall be seven weeks, and threescore and two weeks; the street shall be built again, and the wall, even the troublous times.

Luke 2 vs. 1-7

And it came to pass in those days, that there went out a decree from Caesar Augustus, that the entire world should be taxed. And this taxing was first made when Cyrenius was governor of Syria.

And all went to be taxed everyone to his own city. And Joseph also went up from Galilee, out of the city of Nazareth, into Judea, unto the city of David, which is called Bethlehem; because he was of the house and lineage of David.

To be taxed with his espoused wife Mary, being great with child. And so it was that while they were there, the days were accomplished that she should be delivered.

And she brought forth her first born son, and wrapped him in swaddling clothes, and laid him in a manger; because there was no room for them in the inn.

****

Born of a Virgin

Isaiah 7 vs. 14

Therefore the Lord himself shall give you a sign; Behold a virgin shall conceive, and bear a son, and shall call his name Emmanuel.

Matthew 1 vs. 18

Now the birth of Jesus was on this wise; When as his mother was espoused to Joseph, before they had come together, she was found with child of the Holy Ghost.

****

The Massacre of Infants

Jeremiah 31 vs. 15

Thus saith the Lord; A voice was heard in Ramah, lamenatation and bitter weeping; Rahel weeping for her children refused to be comforted for her children, because they were not.

Matthew 2 vs. 16

Then Herod, when he saw that he had been mocked by the wise men, was exceedingly angry, and sent forth and slew all the children which were in Bethlehem, and in all the coasts thereof, from two years old and under, according to the time which he had diligently enquired of the wise men.

****

His Flight into Egypt

Hosea 11 vs. 1

When Israel was a child, then I loved him, and called my son out of Egypt.

Matthew 2 vs. 14

When he arose, he took the young child and his mother by night, and departed into Egypt.

****

His Ministry in Galilee

Isaiah 9 vs. 1-2

Nevertheless, the dimness shall not be such as it was in her vexation, when at the first he lightly afflicted the land of Zebulon and the land of Napthali, and afterward did more grievously afflict her by way of the sea, beyond Jordan, in Galilee of the nations.

The people that walked in darkness have seen a great light; they that dwell in the land of the shadow of death, upon them has the light shined.

Matthew 4 vs. 12-16

Now when Jesus had heard that John the Baptist was cast into prison, he departed into Galilee. And leaving Nazareth, he came and dwelt at Capernaum, which is upon the sea coast, in the borders of Zebulon and Nepthalim.

That it might be fulfilled which was spoken by Isaiah the prophet, saying, the land of Zebulon and the land of Nepthalim, by the way of the sea, beyond Jordan, Galilee of the Gentiles. The people which sat in darkness saw great light; and to them which sat in the region and shadow of death light is sprung up.

****

Christ as a Prophet

Deuteronomy 18 vs. 15

The Lord thy God will raise up unto thee a prophet from the midst of thee, of thy bretheren, like unto me; unto him shall you hearken.

John 6 vs. 14

Then those men, when they had seen the miracle that Jesus did, said, This is of a truth that prophet that should come into the world.

****

Christ the Priest like Melchizedek

Psalm 110 vs. 4

The Lord has sworn, and will not repent; Thou art a priest forever after the order of Melchizedek.

Hebrews 6 vs. 20

Whither the forerunner is for us entered, even Jesus, made a high priest forever after the order of Melchizedek.

****

Christ Rejected by the Jews

Isaiah 53 vs. 3

He is despised and rejected of men; a man of sorrows, and acquainted with grief; and we hid as it were our faces from him; he was despised and we esteemed him not.

John 1 vs. 11

He came to his own, and his own received him not.

****

Christ's Characteristics

Isaiah 11 vs. 2

And the Spirit of the Lord shall rest upon him, the spirit of wisdom and understanding, the spirit of counsel and might, the spirit of knowledge and of the fear of the Lord.

Luke 2 vs. 52

And Jesus increased in wisdom and stature, and in favor with God and man.

****

Christ's Triumphant Entry

Zechariah 9 vs. 9

Rejoice greatly oh daughter of Zion; shout; oh daughter of Jerusalem; behold thy king cometh unto you; he is just; and having salvation; lowly and riding upon an ass, and upon a colt the foal of an ass.

John 12 vs. 13-14

They took branches of palm trees and went forth to meet him, and cried, Hossana; Blessed is the King of Israel that comes in the name of the Lord.

****

Christ to be Betrayed by a Friend

Psalm 41 vs. 9

Yea, my own familiar friend, in whom I trusted, which did eat of my bread, has lifted up his heel against me.

Mark 14 vs. 10

And Judas Iscariot, one of the twelve, went unto the chief priests to betray him unto them.

****

Christ is Sold for Thirty Pieces of Silver

Zechariah 11 vs. 12

And I said to them, if you think it good, give me my price; and if not, forbear. So they weighed for my price thirty pieces of silver.

Matthew 26 vs. 15

And said unto them, what will you give me? And I will deliver him unto you. And they covenanted with him for thirty pieces of silver.

****

The Money is Returned for the Potters Field

Zechariah 11 vs. 13

And the Lord said unto me, Cast it unto the potter; a goodly price that I was priced at of them. And I took the thirty pieces of silver, and cast them to the potter in the house of the Lord.

Matthew 27 vs. 6-7

And the chief priests took the silver pieces, and said, it is not lawful to put them into the treasury, because it is the price of blood. And they took counsel and bought with them the potters field, to bury strangers in.

****

Judas Position is to be Taken by Another

Psalm 109 vs. 7-8

When he shall be judged, let him be condemned; and let his prayers become sin. Let his days be few and let another take his office.

Acts 1 vs. 18-20

Now this man purchased a field with the reward of iniquity, and falling headlong he burst asunder in the midst, and all his bowels gushed out. And it was known to all who dwelled at Jerusalem; insomuch as that field in their proper tongue is called, Aceldama, that is to say; field of blood.

For it is written in the book of Psalms; Let his habitation be desolate, and let no man dwell therein; and his bishopric let another take.

****

Christ is Accused by False Witnesses

Psalm 27 vs. 12

Deliver me not over to the will of my enemies; for false witnesses are risen up against me, and such as breath out cruelty.

Matthew 26 vs. 60-61

But found none; yes though many false witnesses came, yet found they none. At the last came two false witnesses, and they said, this fellow said, I am able to destroy the temple of God, and to build it in three days.

****

Christ is Silent before the Accusers

Isaiah 53 vs. 7

He was oppressed and he was afflicted, yet he opened not his mouth; he is brought as a lamb to the slaughter, and as a sheep before her shearers is dumb, so he opened not his mouth.

Matthew 26 vs. 62-63

And the high priest arose and said to him, answer you nothing? What is it which these witness against you? But Jesus held his peace. And the high priest answered and said to him, I adjure you by the living God, that you tell us whether you be the Christ, the Son of God.

****

Christ is Hit and Spit Upon

Isaiah 50 vs. 6

I gave my back to the smiters, and my cheeks to them that plucked off the hair; I hid not my face from shame and spitting.

Mark 14 vs. 65

And some began to spit upon him, and to cover his face, and buffet him, and to say to him, prophesy; and the servants did strike him with the palms of their hands.

****

Christ is Hated Without a Cause

Psalm 69 vs. 4

They that hate me without a cause are more than the hairs of my head; they that would destroy me, being my enemies wrongfully are mighty; then I restored that which I took not away.

John 15 vs. 23-25

He that hated me hated my Father also. If I had not done among them the works that no other man did, they had not had sin; but now they have both seen and hated both me and my Father. But this comes to pass that the word might be fulfilled that is written in their law, that they hated me without a cause.

****

Christ's Great Sufferings

Isaiah 53 vs. 4-5

Surely he has borne our griefs, and carried our sorrows; yet we did esteem him stricken, smitten of God, and afflicted. But he was wounded for our transgressions, he was bruised for our iniquities; the chastisement of our peace was upon him; and with his stripes we are healed.

Matthew 8 vs. 16-17

When the evening had come, they brought to him many that were possessed with devils; and he cast out the spirits with his word, and he healed all that were sick; That it might be fulfilled which was spoken by Isaiah the prophet, saying, himself took our infirmities and bore our sicknesses.

****

He is Crucified with Sinners

Isaiah 53 vs. 12

Therefore I will divide him a portion with the great, and he shall divide the spoil with the strong; because he has poured out his soul unto death; and he was numbered with the transgressors; and he bore the sin of many, and made intercession for many.

Matthew 27 vs. 38

Then were there two thieves crucified with him, one on the right hand and another on the left.

****

Christ's Hands and Feet are Pierced

Psalm 22 vs. 16

For dogs have compassed me; the assembly of the wicked have enclosed me; they pierced my hands and my feet.

John 20 vs. 27

Then he said to Thomas, reach forth with your finger, and behold my hands; and reach out your hand and thrust it into my side; and be not faithless but believing.

****

Christ is Insulted and Mocked

Psalm 22 vs. 6-8

But I am a worm and no man; a reproach of men and despised of the people. All those that see me laugh me to scorn; they shoot out the lip, they shake the head saying, He trusted in the Lord that he would deliver him; let him deliver him seeing he delighted in him.

Matthew 27 vs. 39-40

And they that passed by reviled him, wagging their heads, and saying, you that would destroy the temple and rebuild it in three days, save yourself. If you be the Son of God come down off the cross.

****

Christ is Given Gall and Vinegar on the Cross

Psalm 69 vs. 21

They gave me also gall for my meat; and for my thirst they gave me vinegar to drink.

John 19 vs. 29

Now there was set a vessel full of vinegar; and they filled a sponge with vinegar, and put it upon hyssop, and put it in his mouth.

****

Christ Hears them Mocking Him with Prophetic Words

Psalm 22 vs. 8

He trusted in the Lord that he would deliver him; let him deliver him seeing that he delighted in him.

Matthew 27 vs. 43

He trusted in God; let him deliver him now, if he will have him; for he said; I am the Son of God.

****

Christ Prays to the Father for his Enemies

Psalm 109 vs. 4

For my love they are my adversaries; but I give myself unto prayer.

Luke 23 vs. 34

Then said Jesus; Father forgive them; for they know not what they do. And they parted his clothing and cast lots for it.

****

Christ's Side is Pierced with a Sword

Zechariah 12 vs. 10

And I will pour upon the house of David, and upon the inhabitants of Jerusalem, the spirit of grace and of supplications; and they shall look upon me whom they have pierced, and they shall mourn for him, as one mourns for his only son, and shall be in bitterness for him, as one that is in bitterness for his first born.

John 19 vs. 34

But one of the soldiers with a spear pierced his side, and there came out blood and water.

****

The Soldiers Cast Lots for His Coat

Psalm 22 vs. 18

They part my garments among them, and cast lots for my vesture.

Matthew 15 vs. 24

And when they had crucified him, they parted his garments, casting lots upon them, what every man should take.

****

None of His Bones Shall be Broken

Psalm 34 vs. 20

He keeps all his bones; not one of them is broken.

John 19 vs. 33

But when they came to Jesus, and saw that he was dead already, they did not break his legs.

****

He was to be Buried with the Rich

Isaiah 53 vs. 9

And he made his grave with the wicked and with the rich in his death; because he had done no violence, neither was there deceit in his mouth.

Matthew 27 vs. 57-60

When the evening had come, there came a rich man of Arimithaea, named Joseph, who also was himself a disciple of Jesus, He went to Pilate and begged for the body of Jesus. Then Pilate commanded for the body to be delivered.

And when Joseph had taken the body, he wrapped it in a clean linen cloth, and he laid it in his own new tomb, which he had hewn out in the rock.

****

Christ's Resurrection

Psalm 16 vs. 10

For thou will not leave my soul in hell; neither will you suffer your Holy One to see corruption.

Matthew 28 vs. 9

And as they went to tell his disciples, behold Jesus met them, saying, All hail; And they came and held him by the feet and worshipped him.

****

Christ's Ascension

Psalm 68 vs. 18

Thou has ascended on high; thou has led captivity captive; you have received gifts for men; yes, for the rebellious also, that the Lord God might dwell among them.

Luke 24 vs. 50-51

And he led them out as far as to Bethany, and he lifted up his hands and blessed them. And it came to pass as he blessed them; he was parted from them and lifted up into heaven.

My Prayer.....Oh great and powerful God, King of Kings and Lord of Lords. How great and mighty are your workings in the heavens and in the earth, from everlasting to everlasting. As I have now read your words which are indeed life to the hearer and bread to the souls of those who trust in you.

May I from this day forward be ever mindful of your teachings. Cause my heart to meditate oh Lord Jesus by the power of your Holy Spirit, on your words daily, from the rising of the sun to the going down of the same. Change me oh Lord, create in me a new heart, filled with love and compassion.

Use me oh God to tell others of your goodness and of your loving kindness towards mankind. And when the time has come for me to leave this earthly home, may I die a peaceful death oh God, and be welcomed into your glorious heaven which you have prepared for me and all the angels and saints which have gone to their rest before me. That I too may dwell in the house of the Lord. Forever and ever…Amen

One Final Word

Now that you have finished reading the words of Christ, you are undoubtedly left with a lot to think about. Where do you stand in your own life relative to his teachings that he has given to us to live by?

May I reiterate on something you have already read? In Matthew vs. 13-14 you read what Christ said about the two ways. He said; Enter in at the strait gate; for wide is the gate, and broad is the way, that leads to destruction, and many there be that go in there at. Because strait is the gate, and narrow is the way which leads to life, and few there be that find it.

In Case you're wondering about this gate, it's not in your backyard. This is Christ referring to himself and his teachings about how we should live our lives. So in reading this we can easily see that many people choose the way of the world and few choose the ways of Christ.

Now let me bring to your recollection the parable of the sower, which you have also read. You may recall that a sower planted seeds. These seeds represented people who had heard and were taught about the teachings of Jesus Christ. And as you have read, out of these individuals only one person out of the group actually received his teachings and made it to the end. That is to say, received eternal life.

We also read in Matthew 10 vs. 22; You shall be hated of all men for my namesake and that he that endures to the end shall be saved. What's all this about being hated and endurance? The fact is that the majority of people do not want to hear or listen to the gospel and its teachings because it exposes the darker sinful part of their lives.

Nevertheless if you embrace Christ's teachings it is a lifelong race, if you will, and it will take all that you have and all that God has to offer, for you to be a strong Christian. Able to make a difference in this world we live in. And what about making a difference in this world?

Let's take a look at another teaching which you have now read. Matthew 10 vs. 32; Whoever therefore shall confess me before men, him will I confess also before my Father which is in heaven. But whoever shall deny me before men, him will I also deny before my Father which is in heaven.

The fact is that people should know that you are a Christian. Christ wants us as Lutherans, Catholics, Pentacostals, Baptists, Methodists, etc., to be planting seeds about him in this lifetime for his glory. But it's not fun and games.

Let me introduce you to a couple of writings which the apostle Paul put to paper in another portion of the bible. The book of Romans chapter 1 vs. 16; Paul states; For I am not ashamed of the Gospel of Christ; for it is the power of God unto salvation.

Lets now take a look at what Paul's life as a Christian was like after embracing this power of salvation. And what happened to him after the blinding conversion experience, which you read about earlier, that he had on the road to Damascus.

In the book of Second Corinthians chapter 11 beginning in verse 24 we read; From the Jews five times I received thirty nine lashes. Three times I was beaten with rods, once I was stoned, and three times I was shipwrecked spending a night and a day in the deep. On journeys often, in the perils of water, in the perils of robbers, in perils of my own countrymen, in perils by the heathen, in perils in the city, in perils in the wilderness, in perils of the sea and of false brethren.

In weariness and painfulness, in watchings often, in hunger and thirst, in fasting often and in cold and nakedness. What do you think? It doesn't sound to me from the lips of Paul that the calling to be a follower of Christ is necessarily a pleasure cruise does it?

I could go on and on. However that's what you should do for yourself and your own eternal future should you make the choice to embrace Jesus Christ and his teachings. That being said let me leave you with one final writing from the apostle Paul in a letter he wrote to Timothy telling him about the last days of mankind. Tell me if you think this sounds familiar.

This is from the Second Epistle of Paul to Timothy chapter 3 vs. 1; This know also, that in the last days perilous times shall come. For men shall be lovers of their own selves, covetous, boasters, proud, blasphemers, disobedient to parents, unthankful, unholy. Without natural affection, trucebreakes, false accusers, incontinent, fierce, despisers of those that are good. Traitors, heady, highminded, lovers of pleasure more than lovers of God. Having a form of godliness but denying the power thereof; from such turn away.

****

The End Times

We begin with another passage you have read from The Gospel of Saint Mark chapter 13 beginning in verse 5.This begins after the apostles had asked Christ when the end would come. And Jesus answering them began to say; Take heed that no man deceives you.

For many shall come in my name, saying, I am Christ; and shall deceive many. And when you shall hear of wars and rumors of wars, be not troubled; for such things must need be; but the end shall not be yet. For nation shall rise against nation, and kingdom against kingdom; and there shall be earthquakes in many places and there shall be famines and troubles; these are just the beginnings of sorrows.

Also from the book of First Thessalonians chapter 4 beginning at verse 14; we read; For if we believe that Jesus died and rose again from the dead, even so those who have died which sleep in Jesus God will bring with him. For this we say to you by the word of the Lord, that we which are alive and remain at the coming of the Lord shall not precede those which have gone before us.

For the Lord himself shall descend from heaven with a shout, and with the voice of the archangel and with the sound of the trumpet of God; and the dead in Christ shall rise first. Then we which are alive shall be caught up together with them in the clouds; to meet the Lord in the air; and so shall we ever be with the Lord.

****

Counting the Cost

When we read the parable of the pearl of great price. A certain man was digging in a field and unearthed a pearl that was in his estimation worth all that he had. Afterall we were told he put the pearl back, went home, and sold all of his worldly possessions in order to purchase that field, and in so doing, purchasing the pearl.

The pearl of great price spoken about by Christ is in reality the Kingdom of Heaven. Remember Jesus telling the rich young ruler who desired to follow him; Go and sell all that you have and give it to the poor. Then take up your cross and follow me.

****

The Death of the Apostles

Entering into heaven will cost you something even though the gift itself is free. And for some through the years it cost them their very lives. My desire here is to document for you briefly how some of the apostles met their end on this earth. Keeping in mind these are men who lived with, slept and ate with Christ.

Peter: Preached predominantly in Antioch and Rome, where he was crucified for the gospel around 64 or 65 A.D.

James: Preached in Samaria, Judea and in Spain. He was put to death in 42 A.D.

Andrew: Preached in Greece, Ephirus and Scythia. He was crucified in Patras Greece around the year 70 A.D. on a crucifix made in the form of an X.

Philip: Preached in Phrygia and possibly France. He was crucified and stoned in Phrygia about the year 80 A.D.

Thomas: Preached the Gospel in Parthia and India, where he was martyred near Madras being run through with a lance after being stoned.

Bartholomew: Preached the Gospel in Arabia, India and Asia Minor. He was flayed alive and beheaded.

James: He ruled over the church in Jerusalem and also wrote one of the Epistles. In 62 A.D. he was flung from the top of a tower to his death.

Matthew; Preached in a variety of locations in the East and met a martyrs death.

Jude: Wrote an Epistle and preached in Armenia. He was beheaded after being clubbed.

Simon: Preached predominantly in the Far East and was martyred in Persia.

Are You Ready?

Breinigsville, PA USA
16 June 2010
240045BV00001B/65/P